Waterford: An Irish Art

Text / Ida Grehan

Principal Photography / Terry Murphy, A.I.P.P.A. & David Howe

Additional Photography / Walter Pfeiffer & Louis Peterse

Illustrations / Noel Cusack

Project Coordinator / Rose Mary Craig

Creative Consultant / Harry Pesin

Research Consultant / Angie Miller

A Robert Campbell Rowe book

Portfolio Press / Huntington, New York

Author's Acknowledgements

I wish to thank the following persons and organizations for their assistance: the directors and staff of Waterford Crystal, the Southeastern Regional Tourism Organization, Ltd., the National Library of Ireland, Bray Library, Royal Dublin Society Library, Miss Mairead Reynolds of the National Museum of Ireland, Mr. Michael Robinson of the Ulster Museum, Mrs. Mary Boydell, and Sotheby's (Ireland), Ltd.

—Ida Grehan
Enniskerry, June 1981

Design by Anthony Russell
Associate Designer: Barbara Casado

Ireland

Rathlin Island

Carndonagh
Fahan Mura · Coleraine
· Broighter
Londonderry

Inishkeel · Portnoo

LOUGH NEAGH

Bangor

Castlederg

Belfast

Ballyshannon Bay
Inishmurray

Donaghmore

Devenish Island

Loughnashade
Armagh

Downpatrick

LOUGH ERNE

Tedavnet

Sligo

Clones

Ballymote

Killycluggin

Kilnasaggart

IRISH
SEA

Keshcarrigan

Cornalaragh

Ballintober · Castlerea

Mellifont Abbey ■
Kells ·
Newgrange

Drogheda
· Bettystown
Fourknocks

Castlestrange
Cong · · Moylough

Templecross

Annaghdown
· Attymon
· Turoe

Ross
Athlone
Clonmacnoise
· Derrinboy

Tara

Lagore

Lambay Island

BOYNE R.

Dublin ·
Kilmainham

Monasterevin

ATLANTIC
OCEAN

Aran
Islands

Glendalough

Wicklow

Gorteenreagh
Mooghaun North ·

Inis
Celtra

SHANNON R.

Roscrea
Ardcrony

Aghaboe
Durrow

AVOCA R.

Kilkenny

Mouth of the Shannon

Ballylongford
· Ardagh

Holycross
Limerick
Lough Gur
Tipperary

Cashel
Killamery
Ahenny

Wexford

Illauntannig

Tullylease

SUIR R.

Waterford

ST. GEORGE'S CHANNEL

Lismore
Dungarvan

Skellig

Garryduff
Cork ·
· Garranes

0   10   20   30

Contents

The evolution of artisan skills through the centuries viewed in the perspective of Irish social and economic history. Glassmaking is traced from its earliest days in Ireland, with particular emphasis on activity in and around the town of Waterford. Waterford Glass first appeared as a company in the 1700's, experienced successive triumphs and tribulations, disappeared in the mid-1800's, and was ultimately resurrected in this century to become a thriving crystal company.

A photographic essay with detailed information on how raw ingredients are turned into sparkling crystal. Each step is carefully explained, with special emphasis on blowing and cutting, which is done wholly by hand. Blowing teams are seen in action around the fiery furnaces, then the newly-made crystal goes into the cutting rooms, where specialist teams perform flat and wedge cutting as well as copper-wheel engraving.

Over the years Waterford Crystal has created 41 stemware patterns, better known as suites. In 1981, 36 of these are available to the public; the others have been retired. This color portfolio contains all 41 suites in newly-created photographs. Representative pieces from each suite are included.

The history of the town of Waterford and the surrounding countryside from ancient times to the present. While the city is ancient, it is only in comparatively recent times that the county was formed. Although now best known for the crystal made there, the port of Waterford played an important part in Irish history. The nearby towns, villages, castles and coastline also have a romantic and colorful past. Newly-commissioned photographs and illustrations convey the atmosphere of the area today.

Collectors particularly prize both the limited edition and unique crystal pieces. The limited edition series began in 1971. All are cut-crystal vases featuring engraved figures taken from the Bible and the works of William Shakespeare. Each piece is numbered. The master cutter pieces are unique one-of-a-kind works of art. Each master cutter periodically takes time off from his regular responsibilities to create unique pieces that follow no set pattern. They are signed by the cutter.

All of the crystal made at Waterford not belonging to one of the stemware suites comes under the general classification of "fancies." This includes several hundred items ranging from the unusual, such as chess sets, crystal slippers and even a cowboy boot, to the everyday table pieces such as salt and pepper shakers, cream and sugar sets, bowls and vases of all sizes, various shaped decanters and many other crystal objects. Because of the great number of pieces involved, a limited number are shown on a purely representational basis.

A special selection of architectural-style photographic studies of important rooms around the world containing Waterford chandeliers and other lighting fixtures. The rooms and buildings themselves are described. Included are Westminster Abbey, Dublin Castle, the Kennedy Center for the Performing Arts, the National Museum of Ireland and others.

This concluding chapter centers on the special Waterford trophies and other pieces of the famous crystal presented to famous personalities all over the world. The realms of sport, science, the arts, industry and government are all represented.

Introduction

The inspiration for this book came several years ago when I was visiting Ireland. Browsing through what was reliably said to be the 'definitive' book shop in Dublin, I asked for a book on Waterford crystal. None was available. Subsequently, I discovered that there was a very scholarly work, then out of print, about all Irish glass, but only a thin volume about Waterford which the company had sponsored. While the latter was commendable in its presentation of the company's history, there were only a limited number of photographs. Moreover, what I craved was not only a book of facts, but a true art book that would serve as a visual history as well.

In 1980 the decision was made to begin creating this book. From the start, the intention has been to assemble something more than a book; if possible, to publish a portfolio of photographs that, in many cases, would show Waterford crystal in actual size. This meant using a large format, the best paper and printing available, and special attention to design, with collectors rather than curators in mind. It also meant selecting a writer who knew about Ireland as well as about glass. Fortunately, the very able Ida Grehan was available for this project. For the major undertaking of photography, it was necessary to use several individuals, led by Waterford's own Terry Murphy.

It quickly became apparent that we could never hope to show all of the antique or contemporary pieces ever made by Waterford. There are simply too many. In the case of old crystal, there is the additional problem of attribution because few pieces were ever marked or signed. Thus an important decision was reached to show the best representation of Waterford crystal possible without making the book look like a catalog.

In editing all of the written material, it was decided to establish a tone that would hopefully appeal to readers everywhere who share the English language. Since we knew in advance that most of the readers would be outside of Ireland, an editorial decision was made to include a certain amount of historic background that would put the Waterford story in perspective for those unfamilar with Irish history.

In finally putting together all of the pieces of this project, it becomes clear that there are inevitable gaps in much of the early history of Irish glass and Waterford crystal because of the general absence of records, archives and attributable sources. It is hoped, therefore, that the appearance of this book will lead to new discoveries that may be added in a future edition.

Robert Campbell Rowe
New York City, 1981

Irish Crystal & Glass

Prologue

Tracing the origins of Waterford*crystal, one promptly discovers that its history is rife with moments of glory. From its earliest beginnings in the ancient Irish city of Waterford, the record of events speak clearly of a transcendent art form.

Witness the fact that Westminster Abbey commemorated its 900th anniversary with the installation of 16 Waterford chandeliers that now hang from its historic ceilings.

Note that the Irish town of New Ross commissioned an engraved Waterford Crystal bowl to present to President John F. Kennedy on his much-heralded trip to Ireland.

Consider that a Waterford trophy was accepted by a Nobel Laureate for his pioneering work in immunology.

It is true that the great museums of the world seek Waterford pieces for permanent exhibit.

Today, there is perhaps only one continent on which Waterford crystal is not to be found, and that is Antarctica. But behind its global presence still stands the Irish city of Waterford. Here is where the art form began more than two centuries ago. Then, as now, one name gained a pre-eminence: Waterford. To understand and appreciate its origins, it is perhaps necessary to review the Irish past.

Claret Decanter. This elegant piece is probably one of the most widely recognized of the period piece collection. It is made now as it was originally from an old working mold that survived from the first factory back in the late 18th century. The application of the handle alone requires a specialized craftsman.

The unusual details of the pedestal foot, long curved handle, and tall fully-cut stopper set this decanter apart from any other.

*WATERFORD is a registered trademark owned by Waterford Glass Limited, Kilbarry, Waterford, Ireland.

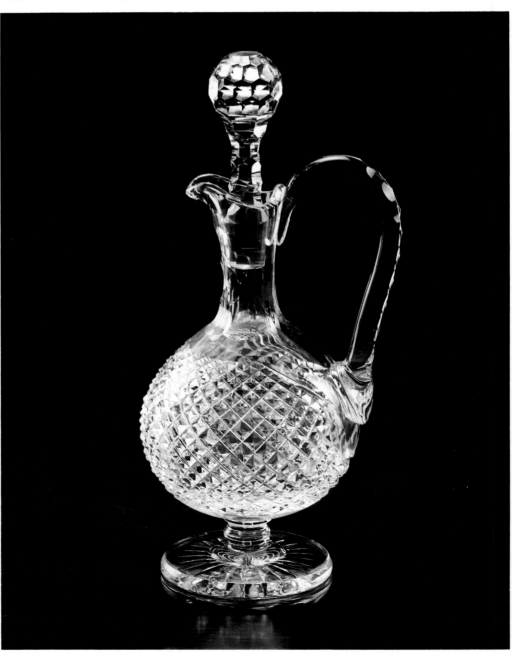

Early Irish Arts

The island of Ireland is small, compact 35,595 square miles (84,421 sq. kms.) with a total coastline of 1,970 miles (3,169 kms.). In area, it is approximately the size of the state of Alabama in the U.S.A. In the 1980s, it has one of the fastest growing populations in Europe. Five million people—in the Irish Republic and Northern Ireland—share its mild, damp climate.

For many years, Ireland's contribution to the history of Western art was largely unrecognized by people outside of the Emerald Isle. In 1977, an event took place that helped change this oversight, especially among Americans.

Following much domestic controversy and soul searching, generated by nervousness about their safety, a collection of Ireland's priceless antiques was gathered from museums, meticulously packaged, and sent off on a tour of the United States with a prestigious entourage both academic and diplomatic. It was headed by Professor F.S.L. Lyons, Provost of Trinity College, Dublin, author of many books on Irish history.

Treasures of Early Irish Art: 1500 B.C. to 1500 A.D. was a collection of Ireland's most precious possessions, including the Book of Kells, the Ardagh Chalice, and the Tara Brooch. It was a richness of ancient art coming from Ireland that had never before been seen abroad. In the cities where the exhibition was shown—New York, Boston, San Francisco, Philadelphia and Pittsburgh—massive crowds lined up to get in. At the Metropolitan Museum in New York, for example, the exhibition's popularity rivaled that of the antiquities excavated from the tomb of Tutankhamen.

This tangible demonstration that the arts had indeed flourished in Ireland for thousands of years came as an enlightening surprise for those who had little knowledge or even awareness, of this remote island west of Britain whose westerly neighbor across the Atlantic is America.

It is a revelation, for example, to realize that around the year 1500 B.C., while Egyptians were fashioning exquisite ornaments for Tutankhamen's tomb, Bronze Age newcomers who came from Europe to Ireland had already settled for several generations and were making intricate gold discs and necklaces, and other metal jewelry which were part of the *Treasures of Ireland* exhibition.

The Coming of the Celts

One point on which historians agree is that the people of Ireland are the oldest settled race north or west of the Alps. Tradition has it that they came first from Spain and were known as Milesians. From the midlands of Europe came the Celts, who escaped from warring Europe to conquer Britain and Ireland which is, today, the last wholly Celtic nation. They called themselves the Gaelic Celts while the Romans called them the Scots, which through the centuries has led to some confusion, especially in Europe. They called their new country Erin, or, in the Latin language, Hibernia.

Although the Celts were a pure race they had not come to a country lacking in culture. The religion of the Neolithic Irish was Druidism. They had built many sacred places for their deities and their dead, as well as great fortresses, many of them still standing. Notable among these is Tara in County Meath where the kings were inaugurated. These early Irish had their own laws, music, poetry and crafts.

The Gaelic Celts were able to conquer Ireland so easily because of their superior weapons of iron, unknown to the natives who had only the noble metals: gold, silver, and bronze. By bringing their knowledge of ironworking to Ireland, the Celts greatly strengthened both its defenses and its economy.

Although no Roman soldier had ever come to Ireland, there was trade between Ireland and Roman Britain and there were also raids for plunder and for slaves. It is said that this is how Patrick, as a boy, first came to Ireland from which he eventually escaped so that he could prepare himself for the priesthood and return to conquer it spiritually by bringing the country into the Christian fold early in the fifth century.

The First Glassmakers

Archaeologists have discovered pieces of millefiori (literally 'thousand flowers') glass at Garranes in County Cork which suggests that glass was being produced as early as the sixth century A.D. In Westmeath, they have found rods or canes of different colors which, when fused together and sliced into thin squares or circles, make millefiori glass. This ancient art probably came originally from Italy. The glass was sunk into wire-thin patterns decorating bracelets, brooches, and later, chalices and book shrines, giving them a rich, jewelled effect.

Although Ireland contained deposits of gold and silver, and made bronze, there were no precious stones, no rubies, diamonds or sapphires. It was the delicate use of glass that adorn the early Irish

The famous Tara Brooch.

treasures. The silver and gilt Tara Brooch is sumptuously decorated with inset studs of amber and glass.

Before being included in the *Treasures of Ireland* exhibition, the Tara Brooch was sent to the British Museum in London for restoration. There it was discovered that the insets, in the form of human heads, were not (as previously believed) of amethyst—one of the few semi-precious Irish stones—but were, in fact, made of molded purple glass.

The silver Ardagh Chalice has often been described as "the finest piece of eighth century metal work that has ever come to light." Here masterful design, technical proficiency of the highest order, and a wide range of materials have been combined to create a work of perfection. Of silver, bronze, and gold, it is incrusted with rock crystal and square blocks of blue glass.

The opening page of St. Luke's Gospel, the Book of Kells.

Although the Christian church had prohibited the burial of valuables with the dead, thus depriving future generations of some priceless glass relics, it did encourage the use of stained glass in church windows. In an age when most people everywhere were illiterate, these windows were actually regarded as sermons in stained glass. Fortunately, the artists who left this glorious legacy provided inspiration for following generations to treasure.

The barbarians who had extinguished the Roman Empire had also brought on the Dark Ages, so Ireland's remoteness proved to be a stroke of good fortune not just for its own inhabitants but for others throughout Europe.

Seats of learning remained throughout the country. Ruined, or sometimes restored, they are still a striking feature of the Irish landscape. From these houses, which were both religious and lay, Irish monks, nuns, and scholars went in waves to Europe where they founded monasteries which became the almshouses, inns, hospitals, and schools of Christendom.

To France and Spain and Italy, to Germany and Austria, even to the borders of Russia they traveled. Luxeul, Bobbio, Cologne, Ratisbon, and Vienna were a few of the famed centers of these "Monasteria Scotorum," as the string of religious houses were called in Europe.

The Viking Period

The wealth of the Irish monasteries caught the sharp eyes of the ferocious Viking mariners who swept down from Scandinavia in their long boats to pillage the rich craftsmanship of Celtic Ireland. It was during this period that many treasures were lost forever. Although books, fabrics, jewelry and holloware were hidden—frequently buried in fields—only a few fragments discovered in recent times are left to remind us of this golden age of Irish art. On the other hand, museums in Stockholm and other Scandinavian cities do have a selection of the treasures of Ireland collected by their adventuring forebears.

The Vikings who finally settled in Ireland proved not to be a total disaster. They introduced coinage, set up markets for trading, developed ports and laid the foundations for what would become Ireland's most important cities, including Dublin, Cork, and a place the Vikings referred to as "Vadrefjord," known today as Waterford.

The Ardagh Chalice with glass insets.

The Vikings also contributed their own style of ornamentation: sinuous animals which twine themselves through the script of books, and on brooches and metalwork. Eventually the tyranny of the Norsemen was broken by Irish warriors led by King Brian Boru at the Battle of Clontarf in 1014 A.D.

The Norman Conquest

Following the departure of the militant Norsemen, Ireland enjoyed a century and a half of comparative freedom, though little peace. There was a relentless power struggle between the leading families who aspired to the high kingship over the four provinces of Munster, Ulster, Leinster and Connacht.

Having conquered Britain, the Normans, together with their English compatriots, arrived in Ireland at Baginbun near the former Viking port of Wexford, not far up the eastern coast from Waterford.

The new invaders' great objective was land. To get it they used every wile, both aggressive and diplomatic. The Normans shrewdly integrated with the Irish, marrying into the wealthy aristocratic families. Like the Irish, they were religious minded and they assuaged their consciences for many a bloody deed by contributing to the restoration of the monasteries. With a view to ensuring a high place in Heaven, they built abbeys and churches. They also built strong, stone castles. Architecture flourished, and many of the native Irish arts were largely supplanted by the burgeoning cultural renaissance that overflowed from Continental Europe.

It was almost certainly the Normans who first brought glassmaking to Ireland as an industry rather than an art. The earliest record of glassmaking dates back to 1258, to "William the Glassmaker" who, it is supposed, came from Normandy in the wake of the Norman conquest of England. During the following three centuries no further reference to glassmaking has been found, yet surely the Anglo-Normans, who were such ardent builders, would have used it at least in their castles and abbeys.

Trouble and Strife

Conflict between the newcomers and the natives was inevitable. Unrest spread through the country. For the native Irish, who still adhered to their own language, customs, and legal system (the Brehon Laws), there was a great deal of harassment. The English overlords soon realized that the Anglo-Normans were integrating too rapidly into the Irish nation. Something had to be done. At the old Irish capital of Kilkenny, in 1366, the English enacted the Statutes of Kilkenny. The Anglo-Normans were forbidden to use or live by the Brehon Laws, to marry an Irish person, or even to dress like them! They could not sell horses or armor to the Irish and they were required to use English surnames and the English language exclusively. They were also forbidden that most insidious of indulgences, the company of Irish minstrels, poets and story-tellers.

Ardagh Chalice: Detail.

Although these statutes were in force for 300 years, they failed, on the whole, to prevent the integration of the two cultures. In fact, the Normans became so much a part of Ireland they produced outstanding soldiers and statesmen. A prime example is the FitzGerald family and its Garret Mor, the Great Earl of Kildare who, from 1477 until his death in 1513, was regarded by the Irish as their real king. His castle at Maynooth was richly furnished with fine objects including books and manuscripts.

In dramatic succession the Irish and the Anglo-Irish won and lost many battles against the English, who were always fearful of Ireland being used as a jumping off ground for the invasion of their country by whatever army they happened to be in conflict with, France and Spain in particular.

When Henry VIII declared himself head of the Church of England he also proclaimed himself King of Ireland and head of the Church of Ireland. To this day, it still surprises many foreign visitors to discover that the Church of Ireland is linked to the Church of England, not the Roman Catholic Church. Henry also suppressed the Irish monasteries as he had done in England. It marked the beginning of a longstanding rift over religion.

In 1602, the Spanish came to the help of the Ulster earls O'Neill and O'Donnell, hoping to drive the English out of Ireland at Kinsale, a port near the southern tip of the country. Instead, the Irish suffered a bitter defeat which was followed five years later by what has been picturesquely described as the "Flight of the Earls" when O'Neill and O'Donnell and many other Irish nobles went into permanent exile abroad.

Because of their close proximity, there had always been much commerce between Scotland and Ulster. Now that many of the Irish leaders there had fled, it was an opportune time to "plant" Ulster with settlers from Scotland. The English did this extensively in 1607.

In 1641, and again in 1646, the native Ulster chieftains, led by Owen Roe O'Neill, tried to drive the planters from their territories. At the time, there was a civil war in England. Charles I was executed, leading to the rise of Oliver Cromwell. The army of zealots led by Cromwell came to Dublin in 1649 prepared to do battle with the "papists." The Irish and their allies were far from efficiently armed or united to oppose this determined crusade. Cromwell stayed a year and then left behind an army which devastated the country and the people.

With the return of the Stuarts to the English throne the Irish saw hope for peaceful times. Then James II lost his throne to William of Orange. The last gasp for James was the Battle of the Boyne in 1690, where the Irish were completely defeated. James went off to France, where the battle had been viewed more in the context of a European power struggle than as a fight for Irish independence. Oddly enough (from today's perspective), even the Pope had backed the Protestant Williamite cause.

Another major turning point in Irish history came in 1691 with the Treaty of Limerick, when another mass exodus of the Irish aristocracy took place, this one known as the "Flight of the Wild Geese." Many of the exiles went on to make resounding reputations in the military and government services of Europe and the Americas.

Above: Part of a page from the Book of Durrow. Opposite: A Celtic High Cross.

At this point, a reader might ask, 'what does all of this history have to do with Irish glass in general, and Waterford Crystal in particular?' The answer is simply that an understanding of the commerce and industry of a nation cannot be separated from its political history. In the case of Ireland, it is almost impossible to follow the growth of industry and trade in the era just described without knowing the essential facts about the special relationship that existed with Britain. The next section shows the growth of glassmaking in Ireland against this background.

Glassmaking Comes to England and Ireland

Although glass originated with the Egyptians, it was the Romans who discovered the art of glass blowing. Its use spread through their empire. Even centuries later, it was the Italians who were in the vanguard of glass making. Their delicate and artistic soda glass was the envy of many a European aristocrat.

The center of this art was Venice, a politically potent city-state throughout the Renaissance that also flourished as one of the world's most important sources of artistic skills. Glass making actually was shifted to the nearby island of Murano because of the constant danger of fire generated by the great heat of the glasshouses.

Many of the skilled Venetian glassmakers set up new operations elsewhere in Europe. One of them, Jacob Verzellini, was working in the North Sea port of Antwerp when his glass was brought to the attention of England's Queen Elizabeth I. In 1571, Elizabeth, daughter of Henry VIII, invited Verzellini to make glass in England. Though others were on the scene already, he was offered the first patent for glass. The reaction of the others already present (apparently they were also from the Continent) was to burn down Verzellini's glasshouse. He persevered, however, and established a sound foundation for the rapid development of the artistic side of English glass.

Although Elizabeth's reputation does not stand high in Ireland (she did found Trinity College, Dublin, in 1591 to promote the Reformation), it was this enterprising queen who, in 1575, granted Verzellini a second patent, this one to set up a glasshouse in Ireland. She hoped he would be as successful there as he had been in England. No evidence exists, however, of Verzellini ever going to, or working in, Ireland.

In 1586, a retired captain of the Queen's army, Thomas Woodhouse, was given an option for eight years to make glass in Ireland. An extract from his patent reads:

"Her Majesty considering that the making of glass might prove commodious to both realms and that Woodhouse was the first that with any success has begun the art in Ireland is pleased to condescend to his petition and therefore orders that a grant be made to him of the privilege of making glass for glazing and drinking or otherwise, and to build convenient houses, for the term of eight years, the glass to be sold as cheepe or rather better cheepe than the similar glass in foreign parts."

Captain Woodhouse does not appear to have made much progress, because three years later he sold his patent for £300 to another Englishman, George Longe. Longe was the first non-European to make a business of glassmaking in England. Hitherto, most had been Italian or French. Evidently Longe had foreseen possible fuel

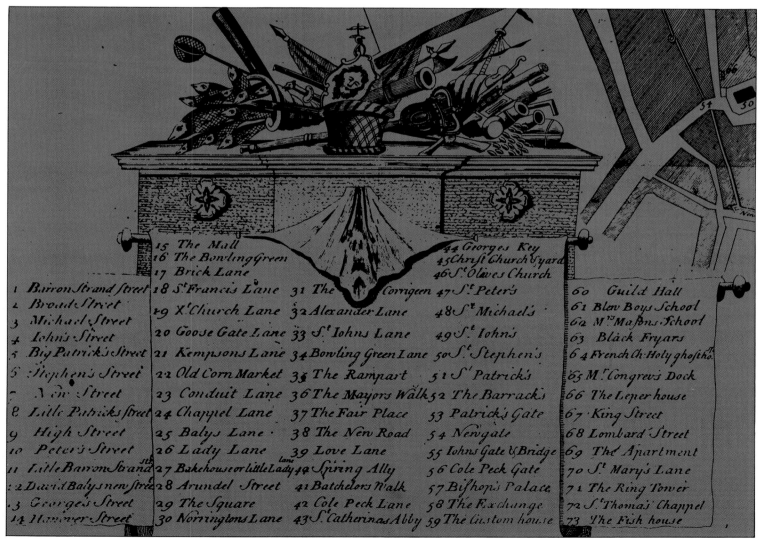

	15 The Mall		44 Georges Key		
	16 The Bowling Green		45 Christ Church Yard		
	17 Brick Lane		46 St Olives Church		
1 Barron Strand Street	18 St Francis Lane	31 The Corrigeen	47 St Peter's	60 Guild Hall	
2 Broad Street	19 X Church Lane	32 Alexander Lane	48 St Michael's	61 Blew Boys School	
3 Michael Street	20 Goose Gate Lane	33 St Iohns Lane	49 St Iohns	62 Mrs Masons School	
4 Iohns Street	21 Kempsons Lane	34 Bowling Green Lane	50 St Stephen's	63 Black Fryars	
5 Big Patrick's Street	22 Old Corn Market	35 The Rampart	51 St Patrick's	64 French Ch: Holy ghost ho.	
6 Stephen's Street	23 Conduit Lane	36 The Mayors Walk	52 The Barracks	65 Mr Congrevs Dock	
7 New Street	24 Chappel Lane	37 The Fair Place	53 Patrick's Gate	66 The Leper house	
8 Litle Patricks Street	25 Balys Lane	38 The New Road	54 Newgate	67 King Street	
9 High Street	26 Lady Lane	39 Love Lane	55 Iohns Gate & Bridge	68 Lombard Street	
10 Peter's Street	27 Bakehouse or Little Lady Lane	40 Spring Ally	56 Cole Peck Gate	69 The Apartment	
11 Litle Barron Strand	28 Arundel Street	41 Batchelors Walk	57 Bishop's Palace	70 St Mary's Lane	
12 David Balys new Street	29 The Square	42 Cole Peck Lane	58 The Exchange	71 The Ring Tower	
13 Georges Street	30 Norringtons Lane	43 St Catherinas Abby	59 The Custom house	72 St Thomas Chappel	
14 Hanover Street				73 The Fish house	

shortages in England. He also cleverly tied political realities to his petition for glass making:

"*At no tyme to contyne above 4 glasshouses in England, whereas there are now 14 or 15, to the great spoile of woodes. But to erect the rest in Ireland . . .*"

Then, after adroitly suggesting that the trees of England could be saved at the expense of those in Ireland, he goes on to point out that a treeless landscape is also preferable: to the woods "*in which the Irish are wont to hide . . . which in tyme or rebellion her Majestie hath no greater enemy theare.*"

Longe's petition was granted and he set up his glasshouse in what is still known as Curryglass near the Drumfenning woods which stretch from Dungarvan (where Waterford Crystal is made today in an auxiliary factory) to beyond the town of Tallow in County Cork. Although Longe is recorded as keeping his glasshouse at Curryglass for 10 years, nothing remains of the house or the wares.

The question of preserving trees arose because of the widespread practice among glassmakers in England, and subsequently in Ireland, of wandering through the countryside and ravaging all of the trees for the heavy demands of the glassmakers' furnaces. This is not to say that trees were a major esthetic concern; as a maritime nation England was constantly in need of good timber for ships to add to the merchant fleet and the Royal Navy.

The result of the restriction on woodburning was a significant innovation in glassmaking: the switch to closed furnaces using coal produced intensive heat, which, in turn, set the stage for Englishman George Ravenscroft to experiment with the use of flint as an ingredient for the raw materials used in making glass. Ravenscroft's flint glass was a heavier and much more durable object than the fragile soda glass of the Venetians. Flint glass was the forerunner of lead crystal and made possible a style of cutting which had never been possible before. It would ultimately have a major impact on glassmaking in Ireland.

Meanwhile, an act of 1615 which forbade the use of wood for the glass furnaces of England was not imposed on Ireland until 27 years later. During this interval licenses were granted to a number of gentlemen of the English nobility to make glass in Ireland. Unfortunately, no glass from this period has survived.

Miniature portrait of Christopher Fitz-Simon, founder of the first glass house in Ireland to manufacture lead table glass. He was in partnership with his brother Richard and a Captain Roche towards the end of the 17th century.

Glass was definitely made in some quantity at Ballynegeragh in County Waterford. There are very detailed records in Marsh's Library, Dublin, for the year 1622 of the profit and loss account of this enterprise which used timber from the nearby forests and *"fyne white clay from Fethard."*

Sales are recorded to the local aristocracy: *"One case of glass to Sir H. Pearse, Baronet; Two half cases to my Lady Viscountess Mountgaret. Two cases of glass to Mr. Byrd of Ballynekell, lawyer for the Lord Esmonde, £2.10.6d."*

Despite this detailed account, no more is known of Ballynegeragh, nor is there mention of the name of the owner. The recorded material does give a meticulous account of the materials, various workers, and the finances of this early enterprise. The reader should bear in mind that monetary comparisons between today's currencies and those of yesteryear are almost impossible to calculate with realistic accuracy. One pound sterling equalled 20 shillings. For the nobility it was not then a great deal of money but for the working man it was. The account reads:

". . . Agreed with Hugh Osborne (founder, consore or maker of the matter and metal of the glass) at 7 shillings wages per week. . and afterwards at 8s. per week if I like well of him and his work, and he to have no dead wages before or without working or after. I say agreed as aforesaid the present 15th of March 1621 and given a 9 penny piece in earnest in the presence of Davy the glassmaker. . . Agreed with the burners of gatherers and bringing in of ashes at 12 penny the barrel. . . for cutting, cropping and cleaving small of sufficient cordes of wood to serve my glass furnace and ovens there at 12 penny the cord."

Thus it can be calculated that the two cases of glass previously mentioned as sold to the lawyer for Lord Esmonde for 2-pounds and 10 shillings represented about five to six weeks worth of wages paid to the factory man Hugh Osborne, mentioned above.

Glassmaking Comes to Waterford

The first record of a glasshouse in the area around the town of Waterford comes from an advertisement in the *Dublin Journal* of 1729.

The glasshouse was probably located by the river Suir near Gurteens, just a few miles from the center of town. The ad proclaims confidently:

"These are to give notice that The Glass-house near Waterford is now at work, where all persons may be supplied with all sorts of flint glass, double and single, also garden glasses, vials and other green glass ware. Sold at reasonable rates by Joseph Harris at Waterford, Merchant."

Two years later, the *Journal* again advertised:

"The Glass-house at Waterford belonging to John Head, Esqr. has been at work for some time, where all gentlemen and others may be supplied with bottles, with or without marks, or at the ware house in Waterford. There will also soon be made there best London crown and other glass windows, and sold at reasonable rates."

One wonders what type of person John Head meant to imply by "others." He himself came from an old Waterford family and his antecedents had been High Sheriffs and Mayors of the city in the 17th Century. He managed the glasshouse for eight years before his death. Unfortunately, the glasshouse died with him.

It was an inauspicious beginning to glassmaking in Waterford. Another 50 years would pass before the art would be renewed there. Before going to that story, however, it is worth considering what was happening in Dublin.

A Wild Goose in Dublin

Captain Philip Roche, a Jacobite and one of the Wild Geese, became disillusioned with the entourage of the exiled James II in France, and returned home to Ireland. Because he was a Roman Catholic, he was forbidden to take part in military or civil affairs which were, at the time, the only true occupations of a gentleman. Roche, who had managed to retain his estate, turned his mind to trade. He had seen some glassmaking during his military exercises in Europe and felt he knew enough to set up a glass factory in his native land.

In the heart of Dublin, in Mary's Lane, he began the herioc effort to construct a glasshouse. Twice it fell down, killing several of the workers and once even nearly entombing Captain Roche. When he thought of building it in the shape of a cone it held firm and soon the fires were burning. The business prospered, and Roche took in two partners, Richard and Christopher Fitz-Simon. Roche died a wealthy man in 1711. Showing concern for the poverty of his country and the people who worked for him, he left legacies to the itinerant traders who sold his glass. He also left a trust fund for the poor and aged which was nullified by the severe Penal Laws which confiscated the wealth of Roman Catholics.

His partners, the Fitz-Simon brothers, carried on the business. One of their newspapers advertisements reads, in part:

"At the Round Glass House on George's Hill . . . are made and making all sorts of the newest fashioned drinking glasses, water bottles, claret and Burgundy ditto . . . bells and shades, hall lanterns . . . all sorts of apothecaries' bottles . . . urinals, breast and sucking bottles. All sorts of tubes, gloves etc for electrical experiments, weather glasses, receivers for air pumps, and all sorts of philosophical experiments . . ."

A wine glass made in 1715 for the Archbishop of Dublin. This is the earliest surviving Irish glass that is dated. From the Hunt Collection, Thomond Museum, Plassey, Limerick, Ireland.

The list goes on, citing "colour workmanship" and "cheaper rates" and then concludes with the statement that *"Constant attendance will be given from eight o'clock in the morning until 9 o'clock at night..."* Obviously, this was a glasshouse that served just about everyone's needs.

In an interview in 1981, Christopher Fitz-Simon, a direct descendant of his 18th Century namesake remembers his father telling him of a cupboard standing in the corner of their home in the hilly country south of Dublin. It was filled with antique glass from the Round Glass House. Alas, someone thoughtlessly climbed to the top shelf to get a glass and brought the whole cupboard tumbling down, smashing the collection so hopelessly that no one bothered to go through the pieces, but simply threw them all away.

The Impact of Parliament on Irish Glass

Students of American Colonial history will appreciate that doing business in Ireland during the 17th and 18th centuries depended heavily upon the whim and financial requirements of the English Parliament. It is not surprising, then, that resentment and rebellion occured on both sides of the Atlantic, and that the source of the problem was frequently economic. In 1639, for example, only a few years after Irish glassmaking started to emerge as a viable new industry, an act of Parliament ordered the end of production. Though this was later rescinded, such acts were hardly an inducement to get into the business of glassmaking. That a few did

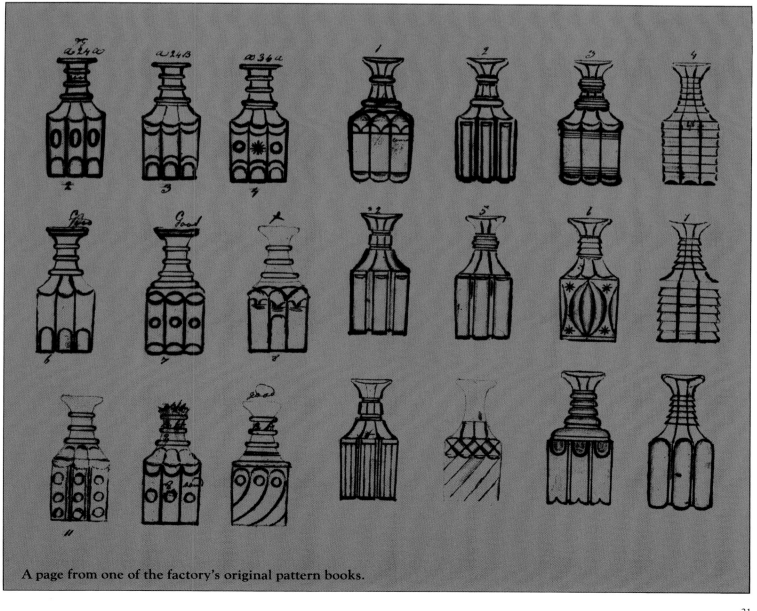

A page from one of the factory's original pattern books.

try, with varying success, is more a testament to determination than entrepreneurial cleverness.

The problem frequently facing Parliament was how to finance a seemingly endless series of wars and military adventures that had engulfed most of Europe throughout this period. As has always been the case, meting out financial penalties on distant colonists was far more palatable than hard-hitting taxes at home.

The Excise Act of 1745

In 1745 the English and their allies suffered a serious defeat at the famous battle of Fontenoy in Belgium at the hands of a French army officered by a goodly number of Irish emigres.

To raise money for the army, the English Parliament passed the Excise Act of 1745. This imposed a duty of almost 10 shillings on each hundredweight of glass used in England and Scotland. For the Irish, however, it was worse:

Whereas the importation of glass into Ireland from foreign parts, and the exportation of glass from Ireland, may be of great prejudice to the manufacture of glass in Great Britain, it is enacted that from May 1st, 1746, no glass of any kind, except glass of Great Britain, be imported into Ireland . . . No glass of any kind is to be exported from Ireland under a penalty of ten shillings for every pound so exported."

This was yet another disaster for Irish glassmakers. They could not export, only import: a ludicrous situation for a poor, small country without any significant domestic market for the luxury of fine glass. The result was a depression among fledgling glassmakers in spite of grants from the Royal Dublin Society (founded in 1731 as an organization devoted to agriculture and culture but best known today for the annual Dublin Horse Show) to try and keep such artisan-oriented enterprises afloat.

Scent bottle, Waterford 1794.

In 1777, taxes in general were increased; on lead glass, they were doubled. The English had their hands full. The American colonies, in revolt, had allied themselves with the French, England's long-standing enemy. British troops, needed elsewhere, were taken out of Ireland.

This created something of a power vacuum, temporarily, at least, in Ireland. The landed nobility decided to raise a force of well-equipped and armed volunteers known simply as The Volunteers. Fearful that the natives might sense an opportunity for revolt, The Volunteers put on a good show of strength with colorful uniforms, banners, and a large number of recruits. For the occasion, a few commemorative glasses were made, including a decanter for The Waterford Volunteers.

In spite of their ties to their social counterparts across the sea in England, The Volunteers accepted Ireland as their country and were greatly incensed at the wealth drained from its revenues to support English wars. They most strongly objected to the restrictions which prevented them from trading with whomever or wherever it suited them.

Led by the Earl of Charlemont from Ulster and the Duke of

Leinster, they pressed Parliament for reform. Backed by the great Irish orator Henry Grattan, who spoke eloquently in the House of Parliament, the right to free trade was reluctantly agreed to by George III in 1780.

Among the celebrators was Jonathan Swift, a dean of The Church of Ireland, who had earlier advocated a ban on all clothing not of Irish manufacture. It was the eminent historian Edmund Curtis, however, who points out another important category when he wrote, "Lord North carried through the British Parliament measures permitting the free export of Irish wool, woolen cloth, and manufactured glass,

Very fine Williamite glass, about 1745. Known as the Cobbe Loving Cup.

Double bottle, probably Belfast c. 1782.

Volunteer Toasting Glass. Dublin, c. 1781.

Fruit bowl. Cork, c. 1790.

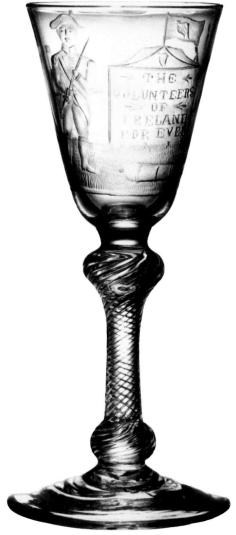

and freedom of trade with the colonies." At last, unfettered by the restraints of Parliament, the making of glass in Ireland was fully open to proper development. It would now be just three years until the historic opening of a lead glass manufactory in Waterford.

A New Era for Irish Glass: the Penroses at Waterford

It had been less than 50 years since the glasshouse at Gurteens, near Waterford, had closed. But after the Parliamentary action of 1780 opening up opportunities in Ireland, the time seemed right to start anew to an Anglo-Irish family named Penrose. Though the site where their factory first went up in Waterford is built over and nothing visible remains today of their effort except a short street marked "Penrose Lane," it was the enterprise of this family and their successors which would have such an impact for generations to come on the appreciation of glass, and create a popular taste for cut crystal which is stronger today than when they began two centuries ago. Over the years Waterford gained a reputation for which so many strive but so few acquire.

The pervasiveness of the Waterford reputation led the late Dudley

Right: George Gatchell.
Opposite: Pitcher and Three-ring decanter, early 19th century.

Westropp, author of the definitive work on Irish glass, to remark, "It is usually said it produced all the old glass now found in England and Ireland."

Perhaps it is because of Ireland's literary tendencies that the country's glass has acquired a mystique which stubbornly lives on. When tapped, Irish glass is supposed to give off a sweeter ring than any other. It is also supposed to be much softer and warmer to the touch than others. Paradoxically, it is also supposed to be tougher and much more durable. A universal myth which defies demise is that old Waterford can be identified from all others because it has a distinctive blue tinge. This may have been because of the absence of rigid controls on raw materials leading to the occasional batch of blue glass. Nonetheless, many an "expert" still swears by the test of blueness.

The stuff of legends was probably not on the minds of George and William Penrose when the two prosperous merchants went about setting up their factory in 1783. To them it was, after all, a business. Although they had no experience in glass, they saw its potential under the new Free Trade Act and they thought Waterford, once the premier city of Ireland, with its splendid quays by the river Suir, the right place to establish their enterprise.

They went to Worcester for expert assistance and hired John Hill from the well-regarded Stourbridge glassworks. He brought with him several skilled workers. Once the factory was ready, an announcement was placed in the *Dublin Evening Post* of October 4, 1783:

"Waterford Glass House. George and William Penrose having established an extensive glass manufactory in this city, their friends and the public may be supplied with all kinds of plain and cut flint glass, useful and ornamental. They are now ready to receive orders and intend opening their warehouse the 1st of next month."

A few years following the setting up of their glasshouse the Penroses petitioned Parliament for a subsidy, mentioning that it had cost them 10,000 to establish and complete, and that they employed between 50 and 70 workers, "most of them brought from England at heavy expense." Shrewdly, they pointed out that since they had been in operation imports of glass had decreased, thus effecting a considerable saving for the Irish economy. They got their subsidy.

They also wooed royalty; according to a 1788 edition of the *Dublin Chronicle*: *"a very curious service of glass has been sent over from Waterford to Milford for their Majesty's use, and by their orders forwarded to Cheltenham, where it has been much admired and does great credit to the manufacturers of this country."*

As Waterford's reputation spread, the nobility and gentry flocked to see the wonders of the glass manufactory. An issue of *Hibernian* magazine from 1790 reported:

"the Countess of Westmoreland, the Marquis and Marchioness of Waterford, the Bishop of Ossory etc. arrived in the city (Waterford) from Curraghmore, and went to see the beautiful manufactory belonging to Messrs. George and William Penrose. Her Excellency took great pleasure in looking at all the various branches of this curious business, and was highly delighted with the elegance of the various articles in the warehouse,

and complimented the proprietors on bringing the manufacture to such perfection."

By this time the aforementioned expert from Stourbridge, John Hill, had left due to a misunderstanding with a member of one of the Penrose families. Prior to his departure, he had befriended Jonathan Gatchell, a clerk in the company. Whatever the cause of the misunderstanding concerning John Hill, it is one of those historic mysteries which will most likely never be unraveled. It is known, however, that Hill passed along most of his technical information to Jonathan Gatchell, including the formulation of the materials necessary for making glass. Thus armed, Gatchell rose to the position of manager.

William Penrose decided to sell. Jonathan Gatchell apparently saw an opportunity present itself, for the next bit of evidence shows him becoming one of the new owners.

A newspaper announcement placed by the new proprietors appeared in a December 1799 edition of the Waterford *Chronicle*:

"Ramsey, Gatchell and Barcroft respectfully inform their friends and the

Right: Water jug, Waterford c. 1820.

Far Right: Three-ring captain's decanter, c. 1850.

Below: Candelabra, Waterford c. 1830.

Opposite: Early 19th century Irish crystal bowl of uncertain origin, photographed in front of a 1735 painting of Waterford city by the Dutch artist Vanderhagen.

public that they have purchased the establishment of the Waterford Flint Glass Manufactory from George and William Penrose, and have opened a shop on the Quay in said concern where they intend to be supplied with an extensive assortment of plain and ornamental glass ware, and hope, by their attention, moderate prices and the quality of their glass, to merit the approbation of their customers.

Then, in an apparent effort to correct what they perceived to be a bad business practice of the previous owners, the ad goes on to state:

"At the same time they hope that no offence will taken be by their refusing to send goods out until paid for. This mode they are obliged to adopt from a knowledge of the many losses sustained by the late proprietors by retailing on credit. Every encouragement will be given to wholesale dealers and exporters as usual. Waterford, December 5th 1799."

New Ownership at Waterford in a Time of Uncertainty

Considering the political state of the country at this time it reflects the commercial tenacity of Jonathan Gatchell that he could advertise so confidently just a year after the whole country, and in particular nearby County Wexford, had been riven by the abortive insurrection

of 1798. It was led by liberal-minded Protestant leaders, including Lord Edward FitzGerald, Thomas Russell, Wolfe Tone, and others, all seeking the legislative independence of Ireland.

Wolfe Tone was one of the founders of the Society of the United Irishmen whose avowed aim was to break the connection with England, "...*the never failing source of our political evils...and to substitute the common name of Irishmen in place of the denomination of Protestant, Catholic and Dissenter*."

He worked forcefully, but fruitlessly towards Catholic emancipation and was strongly influenced by the principles of the French revolution. In 1795 he was forced to emigrate with his family to America. But the following year, like so many of his compatriots, he turned up in France where they persuaded the French to help Ireland.

As adjutant General in the French army, he sailed with an expedition which never succeeded in its intention of landing off the south coast of Ireland because of bad weather. When he heard of the uprising in May 1798, he reached Lough Swilly with a small French fleet that was quickly overpowered. He was taken prisoner and executed.

Bowl and stand, c. 1830, definitely Irish in origin but not marked.

Gatchell and his partners must have been doing something right because they soon moved to larger quarters, this time to a place known as the "Old Tan Yard" in Waterford's Ann Street, while retaining the shop on the Quay.

One of the other partners, Ramsey, died around 1810. In the following year, Gatchell became sole proprietor. It was an impressive feat, from being a lowly clerk to becoming the big boss. In an announcement, he wrote:

Permit me to take the liberty of informing that the partnership lately subsisting under the firm of Ramsey, Gatchell and Barcroft, in the established Flint-Glass manufactory, in this city, has been dissolved on the 19th inst., the term having expired: in consequence, I have purchased the stock of my late partners, engaged the whole of the concerns, and am now carrying on the business, in the same extensive manner as heretofore, intending to use my best endeavours to give full satisfaction. May 20th, 1811.''

In the same year that Jonathan Gatchell took full command of the Waterford Glass Works, Parliament enacted a duty on the export of flint glass from Ireland. It was the beginning of the end for free trade among Ireland's glassmakers and a harbinger of heavier taxation yet

Above: An unusual and richly-cut table garniture set recently auctioned by Sotheby's in Ireland. The set, c. 1830, is described as "a pair of globular jars with covers and mushroom finials, fitted stands, and also a matching decorative centerpiece in two sections . . ." The set is now in the permanent collection of the Ulster Museum in Belfast.

Left: This piece, c. 1820, is called a piggin, a word originally used to refer to a wooden pail with handle.

Decanter, Waterloo, Co. Cork,
c. 1815-20.

to come. But the era had been good for exporters of Irish glass, especially fancy cut and engraved flint glass.

Other Irish Glass of the 1780-1850 Period

Although Waterford became the best-known name among all of the era's Irish glassmakers, several others of note existed. The problem of distinguishing each, however, is the general lack of any hallmarks. This includes Waterford which, except for several pieces carrying the name 'Penrose' or 'Waterford Penrose'—is also difficult to positively identify. Scholars, therefore, tend to hedge many of their hunches by using the word "probably" when identifying pieces. Aside from marks, the provenance of a particular piece of Irish glass is best verified by corroborative evidence such as original invoices, letters, or family histories. When none of this exists, it requires a trained eye to compare glass of unknown origin with what has been already positively identified. For enthusiasts (who are not experts) eager to buy antique glass labeled 'Waterford' or any other old Irish name, there is one word of caution: *beware.*

Celery Bowl, Waterford, c. 1830.

Most Irish glass of the 18th and 19th centuries is referred to as 'Anglo-Irish' glass because of the obvious cross-fertilization between the two countries. This is particularly applicable to cut glass and the heavily ornate Georgian style which emerged from the period in the two countries. The technique used was in the book.

It is simply coincidence that 1783 was also the year in which one of Ireland's other glasshouses opened, also in the province of Munster. This was the Cork Glass Co. of Hanover Street. Fortunately, many Cork glass pieces are inscribed on their base so that identification is possible. The Cork Co. closed in 1818, but another Cork concern, Waterloo Glass House, opened in 1815 and lasted for 20 years. The proprietor, Daniel Foley, seems to have been affected by his close proximity to Blarney Castle, if one is to read the announcement of his opening:

"His workmen are well selected, from whose superior skill the most beautiful glass will shortly make its appearance to dazzle the eyes of the public, and to outshine that of any other competitor. He is to treat his men at Christmas with a whole roasted ox...They have a new band of music with glass instruments, bessons (sic) serpents, horns, trumpets, etc., and they have a glass pleasure boat, a cot and a glass net, which when seen will astonish the world."

It is hard to imagine anyone playing a glass trumpet while standing in a glass boat in Cork Harbor, but neither is there proof today that Mr. Foley tended to exaggeration.

In Dublin, glassmakers were harrassed by demands that they move away from the city's center because of the danger of fire. Among the names that survive are Charles Mulvany, the Irish Flint Glass, Chebsey & Co. and J.D. Ayckboum. The Pugh brothers, whose father had worked for Mr. Foley in Cork, set up a flint glass operation in Dublin in 1852 which miraculously survived for most of the balance of the century.

In Ulster, several glass houses opened in the latter part of the 18th century. Benjamin Edwards, a native of Bristol, came to Ireland to

Right: Covered urn, probably Waterford, made in 1790's, in the Collection of the Ulster Museum, Belfast.

Far right: Large urn, called a wine urn or cistern, made in about 1800 with silver spigot. Waterford. A similar piece was made for the Marquis of Bute. The urn was used for wine or punch.

work in a glass house near Lough Neagh in County Tyrone. A few years later, he went to Belfast and set up his own shop, The Belfast Glass Manufactory. Edwards died in 1812 but the glasshouse continued on under his son's tutelage until 1829. Another Ulster operation, the Newry Flint Glass Manufactory, is recorded as having exported glass to the Carolinas between 1785 and 1790.

Good examples of Irish glass including, of course, Waterford are on permanent display at the National Museum in Dublin and the Ulster Museum in Belfast. There are also collections at the Victoria & Albert Museum in London. In the United States, probably the best glass collection is at the Corning Museum in Corning, New York.

Waterford Under the Ownership of the Gatchells

Although the Penroses got Waterford going, it was Jonathan Gatchell and his heirs who had the longest record of involvement

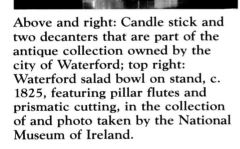

Above and right: Candle stick and two decanters that are part of the antique collection owned by the city of Waterford; top right: Waterford salad bowl on stand, c. 1825, featuring pillar flutes and prismatic cutting, in the collection of and photo taken by the National Museum of Ireland.

with the company. Jonathan himself spent 40 years at Waterford. Little is known about the man or the day-to-day operations of the company, unfortunately, because no complete records survived the period. It is known that Gatchell had to take out a mortgage when he bought out his partners in 1811, and that Waterford employed in that period 75-100 employees (a substantial difference from the 3,000 working at Waterford Crystal in 1981).

Because of the spreading reputation of Waterford during Jonathan Gatchell's tenure, we can only surmise that the company was relatively prosperous. He died in 1823, leaving a widow and three minor children. Prior to his death, Jonathan had made Waterford a partnership, taking in his brothers James and Samuel, and his son-in-law Joseph Walpole. Under the terms of his will, his son George was to come into the business in 1835, the year of his 21st birthday.

In 1825, George IV got Parliament to levy a new excise tax for glassmakers in all parts of the realm. It was the beginning of the end for most Irish glassmakers, though Waterford did survive another quarter of a century.

In the factory, the year 1826 marked the introduction of steam engines to drive the cutting wheels. Business carried on, but prosperity began to fade.

Soon after George Gatchell entered the business he formed a

Above: Decanter, marked Penrose Waterford, end 18th century.

Left: Part of the Hall Collection, Trinity College, Dublin.

partnership with one of the employees, George Saunders. In 1842, they opened a warehouse in Limerick selling directly to the public. The following appeared in an edition of the *Limerick Chronicle* during that year:

George Gatchell & Co. beg to state that they have taken 103 George Street, Limerick, as a branch establishment for the sale of their glass, including cut and plain glass of every description, and every article made of glass for use, luxury ornaments; also, chandeliers, lustres, lamps, hall bells, and candelabra, ormulu and glass. Medical establishments supplied.

By 1848 Saunders had left. In 1850, although he once again sent fancy glass to the Royal Dublin Society's annual exhibit, Gatchell was beginning to despair about the future. In a letter to a relative that same year he wrote that he "...*must now either get a partner with adequate capital, sell, or stop work finally.*" He goes on to note that the company is losing money.

As a final gesture, George sent a most magnificent Waterford entry to the Great Exhibition held in London in 1851. The catalog describes it as an:

"*Etagere, or ornamental centre stand for a banquetting table; consisting of forty pieces of cut glass, so fitted to each other as to require no connecting sockets of any other material. Quart and pint decanters, cut in hollow prisms. Centre vase, or bowl, on detached tripod stand. Vases with covers.*"

By this time, George had decided to give up. In a letter to his cousin Jonathan, he wrote, on April 21, 1851:

I may mention (in private) that I have quite concluded on giving up the business as soon as I possibly can, as I find it quite useless to strive against adverse circumstances any longer. I have tried several expedients to place the business on a better footing by getting additional capital, but in vain.

Above: Center piece, c. 1800; left: two decanters, and left above: two large covered dishes; opposite page, pitcher and goblets. All part of the antique Waterford collection owned by the city.

36

There is a very painful ordeal to pass through and a cheerless future, but I have done my best to maintain my ground and I feel less disheartened at the prospect than I did some time ago. I wish I had the benefit of your counsel in the matter.

Shortly after the London exhibition closed in October 1851, all of the machinery and contents of the Waterford Flint Glass Works went under the auctioneers' hammer. George Gatchell moved to England without, apparently, returning to Ireland. Much later in the century, his old partner George Saunders wryly noted, "*The old glass works are yet standing and have never been taken down since George Gatchell forsook his old establishment where thousands were made in times gone by.*"

But even after its demise, Waterford was the best-known and most widely respected of the Irish glassmakers. Waterford had become a part of the Irish consciousness. Thus, the revival of the Waterford tradition became a collective Irish dream. It would take 100 years before this dream became reality.

By the end of the 19th century the glass and crystal houses of Ireland were virtually extinct. But Waterford remained a living name both at home and abroad, especially in those parts of the world where large contingents of Irish had emigrated. Nowhere was this more true than in the United States, where old Irish glass, regardless of its origin, was often referred to as "Waterford" in the mistaken belief that it had been manufactured by one of the Waterford glass makers. The problem of identification, as explained in the previous chapter, is the general absence of marks. But to the millions of Irish taking root in America and elsewhere the legend of Waterford grew stronger as the years passed. It was Irish pride in an Irish art and with Celtic tenacity, the legend refused to die.

Back in Ireland, Victorian ferment gradually gave way to political discontent. As the 20th century began the twin currents of political and cultural renaissance hit Ireland's shores. The towering literary figure of the day was William Butler Yeats, the greatest poet of his age. The entire Yeats family were enormously talented; his sisters established the famed Cuala Press; his father John and his brother Jack were prominent Irish painters. In the textile arts, the world knew and respected Irish lace, linen and tweed. Notable stained glass was created and, in general, the arts flourished. But crystal, and the name Waterford, remained part of the Irish past.

It was the fire of politics, not crystal making, that burned in Ireland. The Easter Rising of 1916 shook the Irish people into an awareness of the opportunity for their own political freedom.

After a five year struggle, independence from Great Britain was established for 26 of Ireland's 32 counties. Six of Ulster's nine counties became the newly-created United Kingdom province of Northern Ireland. The treaty that ratified this compromise split the people of the new Irish Free State into two opposing camps.

The schism again quickly led to the taking up of arms, this time in a bloody civil war. Paradoxically, two men who would ultimately be instrumental in reviving the tradition of Waterford crystal—Joseph McGrath and Joseph Griffin—fought on opposite sides of the civil war after distinguishing themselves together in the fight for independence.

With the conclusion of the civil war, both sides put down their weapons and began the long process of economic development in a country that, in spite of the richness of its traditions, history and spirit, was essentially a poor agrarian society trying to stand outside the shadow of its richer neighbor across the Irish Sea.

Ireland on its own

It was against the backdrop of world depression and the "gathering clouds of world war" that the Irish set about building their new society. Jobs were scarce and so emigration continued as it had for decades; from a population of eight million in 1840, all of Ireland in the 1930s had less than half that number.

The glass business grew slowly, although at first it was limited to bottles, containers and everyday glasses. In 1932, together with a group of Belgians, Joseph McGrath and his co-directors took over the management of the virtually defunct Irish Glass Bottle Company. As would later be done in Waterford Crystal, the Irish Glass Bottle Company recruited craftsmen in Europe to turn around an ailing company. In time, the Irish Glass Bottle Company would play a vital role in the revival of the Waterford crystal industry.

As with Joseph McGrath and Joseph Griffin, "Waterford" had been a magic name to Bernard Fitzpatrick, a Dublin jeweler and silversmith. He was a regular visitor to European glass factories prior to the war. One of these, near Prague, belonged to Charles Bacik.

A Fresh Start in Waterford

After the war, faced with the Communist takeover of his native Czechoslovakia, Charles Bacik came to Ireland to help set up a crystal factory. Helping persuade him in this decision was Bernard Fitzpatrick.

Initially, the Irish Glass Bottle Company had only a small interest in this venture. Little progress was made until 1950 when through the Irish Glass Bottle Company, with Joseph McGrath as Chairman and Joseph Griffin as Managing Director, there was a revival of the Waterford crystal industry. The company was organized following discussions with Bernard Fitzpatrick, an important shareholder.

For the Irish to recreate a crystal industry in their own country meant starting from scratch. It had been so long since the Waterford and other old flint glass operations had shut down that the new owners faced a formidable task in recruiting skilled artisans. And so they turned to the long-time European tradition of going abroad to find a few key men who would not only produce crystal but who would also teach their skills to the Irish work force.

In 1950, Europe was still ravaged by the destructiveness of the war. There was considerable displacement of craftsmen from Czechoslovakia, particularly from the Sudetenland. The Italian glass

Groundbreaking ceremony at Bally-truckle, site of the 'pilot' factory in the late 1940's. From left to right: Major Cunningham, architect of the Plant; the late Martin Breen and the late Samuel Morris, both of the Waterford Chamber of Commerce; the late Michael Coffey, Mayor of Waterford; the late Cannon M. Barron, parish priest; the next three men are unidentified; Charles Bacik, one of the founders and a director in the company.

industry was also in a depressed condition, with many men out of work.

It was in these circumstances, in the period of 1950-51 that Charles Bacik and Noel Griffin, son of Joseph Griffin and general manager of the reorganized company, traveled to the Continent. They recruited approximately 30 blowers and cutters from various parts of Europe who came to Waterford. At first, they worked in the pilot factory in Ballytruckle, on the outskirts of Waterford, and then in a new factory in nearby Johnstown. The Johnstown operation produced its

Mrs. Bernard Fitzpatrick making the first cut on the opening day of the Ballytruckle factory.

first crystal in 1951, exactly 100 years after the closing of the old flint glass works in 1851.

The 30 craftsmen recruited in Europe trained young Irish apprentices. Though they stayed in the industry for many years, all but one of them have returned to the Continent. Now, the factory is entirely manned by Irish men and women who, in turn, train apprentices.

During an interview in 1980, Bernard Fitzpatrick remarked, "Never in my wildest dreams did I think we would be employing 3,000 people. I think it is one of the finest achievements in Ireland and I am very proud to have played such a significant role in its initiation. It was Joe McGrath's courage, his capital and his good name, and Joseph Griffin's also, that initiated the development of Waterford into what it is today."

Joseph McGrath and Joseph Griffin have passed away, but both Bernard Fitzpatrick and Charles Bacik are still directors of the company. Waterford Crystal today has as its chairman **Patrick McGrath** who, well before Waterford Crystal was re-established, learned a good deal about the glass industry when he worked in the Irish Glass Bottle Company during his late teens. Noel Griffin, mentioned earlier as General Manager starting in 1950, is today Managing Director of Waterford Crystal.

It was during the 1930s and 40s that the late Joseph McGrath became one of Ireland's most successful and best-known businessmen as well as the owner-breeder of several renowned racing horses.

His son Patrick, better known as Paddy, reminisced in a recent interview about his father's early career. He recalled how Joe McGrath (the family name is pronounced "McGraw" in Ireland) was a close friend of Michael Collins, the military leader during the war for independence who was killed later during the civil war.

Joe McGrath subsequently took over the administration of intelligence. In 1922, he became Minister for Labour, and later, for

Top: The Ballytruckle 'pilot' factory.

Above: Miroslav Havel, in the center, with (left to right): Tommy Caulfield, Dan Byrne and Tommy Wall in the Ballystruckle engraving studio.

Left: The first cutting shop at Ballytruckle.

Industry and Commerce. He became disillusioned with politics, however, and in 1924 resigned his seat from the Dail (Irish Parliament). He then entered the business world.

He was labor adviser for the hydro-electric plan designed to harness the waters of the Shannon river. In 1932, with the Duggan family, he founded the financially rewarding Irish Hospital Sweepstakes, the objective of which was to aid the government in the building of the health services, particularly hospitals. Without the Sweepstakes, many of the hospitals in Ireland today would not exist.

The Big Day: founder Joseph McGrath (wearing a hat and rain-coat) arrives in Waterford for the opening ceremonies of the Johnstown factory in 1951, exactly 100 years after the old works had closed in 1851.

Founders Joseph McGrath (left) and Noel Griffin, Sr. shaking hands as present Managing Director Noel Griffin (arms folded) looks on during the 1951 opening ceremony.

One of Joseph McGrath's objectives had always been to employ people, and particularly in the case of the Sweepstakes, to bring people from both sides of the Civil War back together again, and to create vast employment, which the Sweeps did during the Depression of the 1930s, recalls his son.

Joseph Griffin had also worked for Collins in the Independence movement but, as noted earlier, ended up on the opposite side from Joseph McGrath during the unfortunate Civil War. Nonetheless they came together later to contribute their combined talents working for Waterford Crystal.

Like his father, Managing Director **Noel Griffin** is a Chartered Accountant (C.P.A.). In a recent interview he recalls staying with his bank manager grandfather in Dungarvan in the mid-1930s when he was a child. "I was fascinated by the array of old Waterford crystal on the sideboard, particularly the decanters. It was a craft for which we were once famous and there was always this feeling it should be revived," Mr. Griffin said.

"The opportunity to revive the crystal did not come until after the war. It would not have been possible at any other time because only then was there the availability of so many displaced European craftsmen. They were more than pleased to come to the green fields of Ireland and work in the pleasant atmosphere of Waterford.

"When my father sent me from Dublin to Waterford in 1949 to look after the accounts at Waterford Crystal I wasn't qualified yet as a chartered accountant. A few blowers were there then, and Charley Bacik, since retired, and Mirslav Havel, another Czech." One of Havel's first tasks was the studious inspection at the National Museum in Dublin of the old pattern books from the defunct Waterford Flint Glass Works of the previous century. These would be the first patterns, or suites, to be done at the Johnstown factory.

"Through the years Havel has been our chief designer. He's a genius. He can blow, cut, sculpt, paint and engrave as well as design. We still have this very superior man, and we have some good Irish designers who have learned from him."

Noel Griffin then briefly expounded on some of the overall problems of glass design. "You've got to design it to quantity of liquid. The mathematics in the designing is very important. You have to be a draftsman, a mathematician, and a designer. In fact, most of our designers also sculpt, paint and draw; some can blow, others can cut.

Top: Butter cooler.

Above: Footed vase.

"Crystal is special because you're designing vessels to hold a particular liquid; so many ounces for red wine, white wine, less for sherry, more for goblets and tumblers. Apart from their size, vases and bowls are less restrictive. For the designer, these things have to be borne in mind, the thickness, the capacity. The correct size and specifications then have to be attained by the blowers and the cutters."

Turning back to his early days with the company, Noel Griffin reflected on the attempt to sell overseas. "Our first export expedition was to the United States, in July, 1952. I remember my father saying, 'Noel, you can't travel abroad without a hat.' So I had to buy a brown hat for the trip. I never wore one before, but I went off to the States with a hat.

It was a long journey. "We had a 15-hour trip, non-stop on a DC-4, which was the top plane you could travel on then. Usually it went to Gander. Our flight was direct to New York. We got on board about midnight. At eight in the morning, Irish time, Con, who was asleep, woke up and demanded his breakfast. The hostess said, 'There's a subtraction of five hours, it's now only two o'clock in the morning. You're not getting breakfast for another five hours.' Con got very cross. Finally she brought him coffee and cake. That's all she had."

For two Irishmen, it was unfamiliar weather in unfamiliar terrain. Said Noel Griffin, "When we landed in New York it was hot as hell. We went to the Irish Consulate (this was before the days of the Irish Export Board) and sweated away, opening our big crates of samples. We were really keen to distribute our glass.

One buyer walked in and looked. 'It's not blue,' he said. 'You've brought the wrong crystal. It's totally wrong. It will never sell.' Here was a prime example of the blue Waterford myth. We spent three weeks there until eventually we found an agent. Then we went to

Right: Sugar bowl and creamer.

Below: Footed centerpiece bowl.

Opposite: Bowl on stand.

These examples are all contemporary versions of original Waterford designs.

Canada. At the end of the trip the value of the orders we got was a few hundred pounds" (about $500).

Cornelius Dooley, also a director of the company, well remembers the struggles of Waterford's early years. A former diplomat posted in London during the war, Con Dooley, a nephew of Joe McGrath, moved to Waterford in 1950 to take on the responsibility for sales. He met his wife-to-be there and now regards himself and his eight children as Waterfordians.

Con Dooley also recalls a childhood in which the adult talk was often about reviving crystal making in Ireland, and of how, for historic reasons, it had to be in Waterford.

Mr. Dooley's first sales were, predictably, in Ireland. "We began selling to the home market, to all the top Dublin stores: Switzers, Brown Thomas, Arnott's, Weir's, West's, Clery's, others, and also to Maguire & Gatchell, who were then in Dawson Street. They had a connection

with the Gatchells of Waterford Glass of a hundred years ago!

"Noel has already described the many difficulties we encountered on our first trip to New York. Our first few years were very grim, what with the poor reception we were getting from stores throughout the United States and Canada. We couldn't sell to Britain at that time because of their barrier on the importation of luxuries like crystalware. They were exporting crystal to America and nobody was allowed to import," Mr. Dooley remembers.

Visitors Spread the News at Home

Con Dooley

The bright sales spot on the map was Ireland. As Con Dooley recalls, "We sold very, very well on the home market. There were so many tourists coming through Ireland that our name was beginning to spread because they were taking home crystal and the good news that Waterford Crystal was being made again. It was our best advertisement because we couldn't afford to advertise."

Progress was slow. "Little by little, like the stone wearing away, year by year I travelled to America and Canada, once a year, sometimes twice, plugging away and getting very little further each time." he said. "In those days we had neither the time nor the money to travel to places like the West Indies, though through correspondence I set up agencies and our mailed orders were beginning to grow substantially. The orders were pouring in from Altmans in New York, but from elsewhere in the United States they were negligible.

"Meanwhile, of course, our factory was growing. We had started with the experts from Europe and they had trained our Irish boys. So our apprentices had become master blowers and master cutters. As they moved up, they needed more apprentices to 'feed' them. It was an on-going thing. The factory was growing, our production was growing, but we were not getting the orders which would make us completely happy."

The company decided on a change in tactics. "In 1958, we decided to cut adrift from our New York agents and go it alone as we had been doing in Canada," said Mr. Dooley. "We were doing fairly well there. So I started travelling the States saying, 'Now, we're going to sell direct from the factory to you.' I opened up most of the bigger stores there, like Marshall Fields and Jordan Marsh."

Noel Griffin remembers the time vividly. "We decided the agent wasn't being successful. I spent January and February in America. I never want to go again to the northern part of the States at that time of year. My ears nearly fell off with the cold.

"I only went occasionally, but Con went every year. We found, selling direct to our customers was working out better for us. Altman's, where Johnny Miller was the buyer, was our biggest customer. Jack Burke was the president of Altman's and now he has succeeded his father as chairman. With Altman's and the Burkes and Johnny Miller there has been a great history of Irish relations. They really helped us along with Waterford crystal on the American market. It was about 1960 that Johnny Miller resigned and became President of Waterford Glass, Inc., which is our own distributing company in the United States," said Noel Griffin.

The Tide Turns in the 1960s

Con Dooley recalls how events changed. "That started us on the high road. It was the early 1960s. I flew into Shannon one Friday. In those days we worked a 5½-day week so I was in the office on Saturday when I met Noel. 'How did it go this time?', he asked. I said, 'It's no longer a sales problem, it's a production problem from now on.' He didn't believe me, but we took off then. I didn't travel to America for seven or eight years because the Americans flocked to Ireland, guns to our heads. We never had enough crystal for them."

Shaping a stem during the early days, c. 1951.

Below: Tommy Wall, present head of engraving, seen working during the early days of the Johnstown operation, c. 1954.

Noel Griffin then added: "Within a few years we decided we'd have to move. We had filled all the Johnstown acres. In those days we made all our sales, our big impact on the world in that very small Johnstown showroom with the crystal exhibited against the black velvet-draped walls.

"We opened our new factory at Kilbarry in Waterford, in 1970. The factory was built in several stages, the last of which was only recently completed," Mr. Griffin said. "Before this last stage was completed, however, we realized we were employing too high a share of the youth of Waterford. So we decided we'd build somewhere else. We bought land on the coast at Dungarvan (28 miles south of Waterford) and built a factory there where the process is the same as at Kilbarry."

In the winter of 1973-74, a minor set-back occured. Said Mr. Griffin, "We met our first crisis, the oil crisis. It affected the world economy of

Above: This picture was taken in 1954. It shows the members of the company's first Joint Committee. They are, left to right: Tom Kennedy, Noel Griffin, Don Cahil, Anton Schoenberger, Mrs. Josie Tyrell, Bill Dophin (deceased), Umberto Campani, Walther Erben, Rudolph Mulac, Oscar Ilg (deceased), Paddy O'Keefe, and Carl Bacik.

Right: Men from the factory gather for a company meeting at the Shelbourne Hotel in Dublin, c. 1955.

course. We caught the draft and wondered if if we had been too ambitious. It was only a temporary stuttering and we were only worried for a few months before things took off again. The result was we had to plan yet another factory, this time for lighting ware, for which the demand is so great it was impinging on our normal production."

In 1959 the company's management turned to the buyer of their top customer at the time, Altman's in New York, and asked him to head a new company, Waterford Glass Inc. This was to be an American-operated distributor dealing directly with American retailers. The buyer's name was **John Miller,** an American with Irish ancestors. John Miller agreed to the assignment.

"I was 37 years old at the time and had seven children," recalled Mr. Miller during an interview in 1981 in his lower Fifth Avenue showroom office in New York City. "I had no doubts that we would be successful," he said, "but neither did I have any feeling that the task ahead was going to be easy."

What assured John Miller about the future of Waterford Crystal in America was the background he had gained in years of traveling the world buying glass of all kinds. This often entailed long trips to Europe that began and ended on the Hudson River docks where the last of the great trans-Atlantic passenger ships landed. In Europe, the eager young buyer visited virtually every crystal-maker offering wares for export. It was this intensive training that enabled Mr. Miller to develop a keen eye for true quality in crystal. Frequently on those trips he would stop in Ireland because of the orders being placed for Waterford Crystal. He also enjoyed the people he met there, respected their work, and saw an opportunity to combine Yankee ingenuity with Irish crystal.

"In looking back, I knew then it was the factory with the best future. Others were closing down or getting out of quality crystal. Waterford had a terrific labor force, and a great name," Mr. Miller noted.

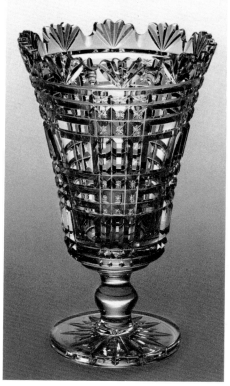

Footed vase (originally a celery dish).

And so John Miller met the challenge with enormous enthusiasm and energy, setting off across America on long selling jaunts. "I made a practice of only going to the top store in each town," he said. "Don't forget, I knew every important glass and crystal buyer in the country." Back home at the warehouse in New Jersey, weekends would find him packing what he had sold earlier. His sister kept the books, and frequently other family members joined in the work.

It all added up to long hours and modest success, but never any loss of conviction on the part of John Miller that Waterford would, indeed, succeed. He also understood the need to advertise, and for this, turned to Harry Pesin, a veteran New York advertising professional. The result was an innovative advertising campaign that is still considered a landmark. "Pesin's contribution was crucial," Mr. Miller said. "His lyrical prose and photography captured the essence of Waterford."

The advertising ignited a crystal fire which burned its way into America's consciousness. "A real turning point was the involvement of the late Lew Seiler," Mr. Miller added. It was early in the 1960s and Lewis P. Seiler was Chairman of Associate Dry Goods, one of the most important retail organizations in the United States. "Lew believed in Waterford, and saw its potential. That was critical to our recognition." As all America gradually became aware of the unique Waterford story, the orders began to flow. Then they started to pour.

Reflections

In the struggle to make a success of Waterford Crystal there wasn't much time for the people working there to linger over the past. During the assembling of this book, however, it became necessary for several persons, especially the founders, to not only reflect on specific events but to expand the thoughts and experiences associated with their time at Waterford Crystal.

"One thing I discovered on my first visit to Europe," said Noel Griffin, "is that we make the most scintillating crystal in the world. We have a brilliance that nobody else has been able to achieve. There's no secret about it, it's the 33% lead content. It is very difficult to maintain quality with so much lead in the glass. To maintain quality rather than brilliance many factories have reduced their lead content to about 24%. Less lead means less problems as regards quality, a lesser rejection rate on the factory floor.

"We were increasing production while many of the European factories were contracting rather than expanding. They were getting rid of their skilled workers, who were discovering that they could get more money in a car factory than by blowing or cutting crystal. When the demand for Waterford Crystal began to grow, when it developed widespread appeal, we, too, were growing. Every prestige store in the United States got interested then. We had to say, give us your orders 12 months in advance and that is the nub of our success."

Con Dooley added, "There's a lot of good luck in that we pinned our fortune to a star, we believed in Waterford, believed in cut crystal, believed it would be a tremendous success one day.

"The beginning of the general use of crystal really started with modern Waterford. Many of the crystal factories that remain—making hand-cut crystal—are very pleased with our success because they are also doing well. There's room for everyone. I've never worried about competition. I'm glad of it. It takes a bit of weight off us."

**Patrick W. McGrath,
Chairman,
Waterford Glass Limited.**

In looking back, Noel Griffin sees the turning point as when they set up their own company in America. "Our handling of the market had been wrong until we got the right company, the right man—John Miller—and the right image.

"I remember the previous people we had distributing our glass—or crystal—I hate using the word 'glass,' it is crystal—they just didn't understand the crystal market which is different from the glass market. Glasses are mere drinking objects." He then added, "'Waterford' is the trademark of Waterford Glass Limited, which produces this prestigious product."

Going back to the theme of glasses as drinking objects, Noel Griffin recalled, "We were told in our early days that Californians don't even use glasses, that they sit all day on the beaches drinking coffee out of paper cups. Today, one of our biggest markets is the West Coast of America." He went on to add that Waterford Crystal is sold in 60 countries around the world.

"I'm Managing Director of our whole group of companies, but specifically of Waterford Crystal. My main interest, naturally, is the crystal company. Having spent 30 years there, the people at Waterford are my consuming interest. It's a people business, not a machine business. Managing our sort of business is really concerned with people, understanding people, understanding trade unions, the outlook of individuals and craftsmen, and making sure we do our best for them. They are the industry. Without them, there would be no industry." Mr. Griffin then noted, with satisfaction, that there have only been three minor and very short strikes in the last 30 years.

He then turned to a favorite subject. "The Irish were supposed to be lazy. We've proved they're not. The people in our factory work as hard as anyone, anywhere. It's not just money, either, it's the motivation. We all have this pride in making something Irish that is excellent. There's a great pride in being an engraver, a blower, a cutter in Waterford or indeed anywhere else in the factory.

Noel Griffin, 1926-1981.

"Many of our people go abroad on holidays, some of them to the United States. It makes them very proud to see Waterford abroad. They deserve to be because they work very hard. They're well paid; we have all the usual social amenities as well as pension plans, sickness benefits, permanent disability funds, everything we can do for the concern of the industry. We always look on it as a kind of co-operation between ourselves, the workers and the unions."

For Noel Griffin, the long, hard days of the early years have given way to a better-balanced life. "I'm not a believer in work alone. I don't play golf. I gave it up when I lost 18 balls after 17 holes. I have no patience for it. I do have patience for fishing. I hunt and shoot and swim, mostly at Dunmore East on the Waterford coast."

No picture of Waterford Crystal would be complete without talking to the craftsmen themselves. What follows, then, are four interviews conducted early in 1981 with four veterans who began their careers during the early years of the company. Appropriately, this section begins with **Miroslav Havel**, the Czech emigre who arrived on the Waterford Crystal scene in its earliest days and subsequently adopted Ireland as his home.

Miroslav Havel is chief designer at Waterford. He came to Ireland in 1947 at the invitation of Charles Bacik, one of the founders mentioned earlier in this chapter who preceded him to Waterford.

During the war Mr. Havel, like his father, was forced to work in the coal mines near his native Prague. As a result of ill treatment then he became deaf in one ear and needs a hearing aid for the other. After the war he was at the University of Prague when what he describes as "the beautiful letter" arrived inviting him to Waterford.

"I thought of oranges and bananas. I was thinking of some tropical country. It was soon after the war and we hadn't seen bananas for eight years," said Havel. Though Ireland has never been labeled a

John Miller

Hold Waterford to the light and you can see faintly etched the signature that identifies it as an authentic work of art.

Each piece of Waterford crystal is a signed original, made by hand with heart. Born in white hot heat, its sheer brilliance reflects the glory of the distant past.

Every single facet is cut by hand in Ireland, just the way Waterford museum pieces were cut long years ago.

Waterford gathers the light of ten thousand yesterdays to illuminate ten thousand tomorrows.

It is an investment in art that will enchant you now; and reward you and your heirs as it grows in value.

Write for free full-color booklets. Waterford, 225 Fifth Ave., New York 10010.

Or visit the Waterford Gallery at the important store in your area.

Isn't it time you started collecting signed originals by Waterford?

(And English bone china by Aynsley, to go with it?)

COLLECT WATERFORD.®

Above: Projecting an image of Waterford as collector's art, this advertisement featured a picture by Harry Pesin, shot in Del Mar, California, in the early 1970's.

Left: One of a series of full-page advertisements that reached millions of Americans in the first decade of Waterford's renaissance.

Write for brochure to Waterford, 225 Fifth Avenue, New York 10010.

A sweet mystery of Waterford Crystal.   into her new home.
                                        Every facet of beauty is cut by hand,
                                        with love, in Ireland, just the way
                                        Waterford heirlooms were cut
                                        distant past.

YES, SAID THE BRIDE. YES. YES.

"tropical isle," the prospect of getting out of war-torn Europe was a great incentive to go to Ireland.

In 1948 the Communists took over Czechoslovakia and he did not see his parents for 25 years. He was a stateless person for seven years until he took Irish citizenship. He married an Irish woman and they now have a family of six children. One of his hopes became reality when one of his children joined him in the factory as an engraver.

Miroslav Havel believes in a constant flow of new ideas. "I am now here 33 years. I know every inch of the factory. But I cannot change my style, so fresh ideas may come from outside. We are getting applications all the time from boys and girls who want to be designers. What they do not realize is that design is not a pure art. Design is a very slow process. You run into a vacuum and don't know which way to get out. You also have to have the sense to design something that can be sold for a reasonable cost," Mr. Havel noted. "It's bad for the designer to be stubborn. You cannot work in the community of a factory that way. You have to consider what the blowers are capable of, the cutters and so on. I have five assistants working with me. Sometimes they go and visit another factory, and they come home full of ideas.

Miroslav Havel in Gladstone Street, Waterford, c. 1950.

"At the beginning I collected the best students at the technical school and taught them there. Now that is impossible because of our size. We take people as they come. We give them a chance to see what it is all about for three to six months. We have training schools in the factory for the cutters and the blowers and during the trial period we find out if they are suitable or not for the work. We are honest enough to tell them it is better if you quit, or, stay because you have the talent. We have a long waiting list, but you have to think of the future all the time. You cannot stop."

Miroslav Havel reflected that "...there's no day without some problems, healthy ones. All in all designing is a very rewarding job. Outside of work I paint portraits when I have time." He then added: "Since I came to Ireland I have always been happy that my name is Havel. It's easy to spell and pronounce, not like some Czech names which play havoc with your tongue. In fact, it's well designed!"

Bobby Mahon comes from a small farm in County Waterford. When growing up and going to school he helped on the land. "Conditions were so bad in the Fifties," he recalls, "that in Waterford it was difficult to get any boys to stay." Bobby Mahon was lucky, he got an apprenticeship as a glass blower. He is now a 25-year veteran and has graduated to the responsible position of Floor Supervisor.

"Working conditions were very difficult in the old days. Space was cramped. You were working close to each other and there was no proper air conditioning and you were working very, very close to the furnaces. Believe me, in the summer you really earned your money. When they built on the new section at Johnstown conditions did improve considerably. Then, moving to Kilbarry (where we are now) we had a completely new industry."

Mr. Mahon turned to a discussion of the blowers' work. "They have a lot of preparatory work to do. They come in about 7:40 in the morning. They're very particular, they have their own wooden tools

Bobby Mahon

Right: Bishop's Palace and Christ Church.

and they like to prepare them themselves. You just don't come in and switch on a button and work away.

"I come in even earlier, at seven o'clock. I clean the glass for the blowers. Otherwise the first half hour of production could be bad due to impurities. We call it cords, stones...various small things may have gotten into the metal. When the crystal has been melted down for a 48 hour period any impurities come to the top. To put it simply, I rake these off with a blowing iron."

Bobby Mahon has spent most of his career working on large pieces such as vases, lamps and trophies. "Most people ask, 'do you need more breath for the big ones?' Not necessarily. Take the big world globe, it may require quite a bit of breath, but only a little bit extra when you're filling the molds. When cold air gets hot it expands so you get the hang of putting your thumb on top of the iron as you cool the glass in the mold. Inside, the air is getting hotter and hotter so it keeps the glass firm against the side of the mold. You've got it naturally compressed. You haven't got to keep blowing."

According to Mr. Mahon, "Rhythm is everything. If the blower goes too far ahead of the stemmer, when he puts on the stem it probably won't break at that stage, but because of the massive difference in temperatures of the bowl and the stem it will eventually not anneal, or knit back properly together, so that it will break again. It requires a lot of concentration. Everybody has got to watch everybody else. There's a lot of team work. It looks very easy. Everything falls into place. It just looks easy because you see four people working together who have been working together for a long time.

"I have a son two years in the factory and he loves it. He did very well at school and could have gone on to college, to one of the professions, perhaps. He'd seen some of his older friends fail to get the jobs they'd expected. So, a few years ago, he came in here during the school holidays to have a try and he liked it and now he's here.

"It's definitely healthy work. I've been here for almost 25 years and I remember years ago, as a beginner, I noticed some of the people who had been around three or four years before. Their teeth were very bad. I asked why, and the reply was, 'when you're blowing the iron as long as we are, your teeth will be bad too.' It worried me terribly. Thank God I've never lost a tooth. I think in every way it's as healthy now as any industrial job can be, and healthier than most. We've got good ventilation, plenty of air conditioning and space to work."

Bobby Mahon is an avid golfer after work hours, though in earlier years he played the rough and tumble national game of hurling.

In looking back, he remembers the times when not everyone was optimistic. "I remember a lorry driver saying that, at one stage, all we're doing is filling every shed and store around Waterford. We'll never, ever empty one again." Bobby Mahon smiles. "That didn't last long."

Michael Ryan

Michael Ryan joined Waterford in 1953. He is now Assistant Cutting Manager. He lives on the coast in Tramore, a 15-minute drive from the factory.

"I came to the job from Technical college," he recalls. "You have to have a knowledge of drawing. You will find that most of our cutters are pretty good at designing and painting. Some of the lads in the cutting are in an art club in the city.

"When we were apprentices we used to have to go back to the technical college one day a week for design. The factory sent us there. Now we have our own training school."

"The apprentices come in at about 16 years of age and they get six weeks as a test period. If they're satisfactory, they'll be put into a production shop for the rest of their training period. We work in teams of six or three, and the apprentice would be attached to one of these teams.

"After three years they do a test bowl. After four years they get a more difficult one. This gets them into the proper frame of mind for the most important test, the five year bowl. If they pass, they qualify. It's nerve-wracking. Takes about a day and a half. When it's over, and they pass, their salary goes up a helluva jump. It's a great incentive, it's their big, big day.

"Ours would be a very traditional form of cutting, generally designed by Mr. Havel or one of his assistants. We try to stick to what would be regarded as a Waterford pattern, a throw back to the old Waterford type. We find that it looks best on our crystal. I would have no doubt in saying that the most popular suite of crystal is "Lismore."

"Recently we have opened a new department, a section where we blow and cut special pieces, collectors' pieces which Mr. Havel designs. Here is another opportunity for the cutter to express himself.

We rotate the job. We allow some of the more senior cutters to do these special pieces."

Tommy Wall is a senior engraver. It is a small, but important, section of the company, with seven qualified engravers and three apprentices. Mr. Wall started at Waterford in 1951.

"There was very little work for school leavers (the Irish equivalent of high school graduates) before the factory opened. You got a job or you emigrated. For me, the timing of the factory's opening was just right. I was able to use my talents. I could draw with pencils, but there was no art training in my school. When I got the job as engraver I went to night school and kept going for a good many years.

"I served my time with Mr. Havel, but my first job when I came in here had little to do with engraving. The engraving machine wasn't ready, but I had all the materials there on the bench, so I put it together. I had to line up the bench, put on the motor, put on the shaft for two benches, and then sit down and work it. In between, I mixed cement and put it on the floors. I didn't mind. I loved it. I really did.

"We have engraved all the presentation pieces for the American Presidents from Eisenhower on. When Kennedy came to Ireland, the nearest he came to us was New Ross, 21 miles away. We did a special vase and it had four different panels: The New Ross coat of arms; the type of ship his ancestors would have sailed from here; the old family homestead in Dunganstown, and the White House. I did two of the panels and another engraver did the other two.

"The work requires enormous concentration...To me a five-year apprenticeship is just the beginning. You have to keep considering all the time. That's why I don't understand what 'serving your time' really means. Normally you serve your time in order to be able to do something. Suddenly, you're able to do it and you can do it automatically without even thinking. But in our job, you can't do that. When you get down to detail it is just as intricate as when you were here for only five years.

"Mostly, we do sports trophies and presentation pieces. Many of these look really spectacular. But engraving is only a small complement to the cutting rather than the other way around," says Tommy Wall. He sums it up neatly by saying, "Waterford is a cut crystal factory."

After hours, company employees quickly scatter, especially in the spring and summer months when long, sunlit evenings mean several hours for sports, hobbies and working outdoors. Most live within a few minutes of the factory, some still maintain farms in the nearby countryside. There is a social club jointly owned by the factory and the workers which has an indoor swimming pool (also available to all Waterford residents), squash courts, indoor mini-soccer, gymnastics, a lecture room, a hall for functions, and a bar. Outside, there are tennis courts, and playing fields for Gaelic games, rugby and soccer, plus a pitch and putt course. Over at the Waterford Golf Club, the men's number one player is a cutter of crystal by trade.

Tommy Wall

Michael Ryan is another one of the veterans who now has a son working for Waterford Crystal. "This is something which has only begun to happen in the last couple of years," he explains. "Up to then the work force was too young to have children old enough for that."

For a visitor to the factory, sitting in the marble-lined exhibit hall where massive chandeliers hang over gently splashing fountains, the present-day success of Waterford is literally dazzling. Light bounces and diffuses from row upon row of stemware, vases, bowls, decanters, lamps, trophies and what seems an almost endless array of other crystal nuggets.

While there is no name better known for crystal than Waterford, a visitor is struck by the open friendliness of everyone who works there and by the lack of pomposity in the attitudes of management as well as their ready kind comments for competitors foreign and domestic.

Miroslav Havel

Waterford is, in a sense, a metaphor for Ireland, sharing its ups and downs, the good times and the bad. Chairman Paddy McGrath sums it up when he says, modestly, "The name of the game is luck, whether horses or running a business. You've got to put the best you can get into it, then hope your luck stays with you. Waterford came on stream just as heavy cut crystal was coming back into fashion. We took advantage of that." He then adds, "Today's patriotism is making your standards come up to what you expect."

Noel Cusack

Waterford Crystal headquarters in Ireland.

How Crystal is Made

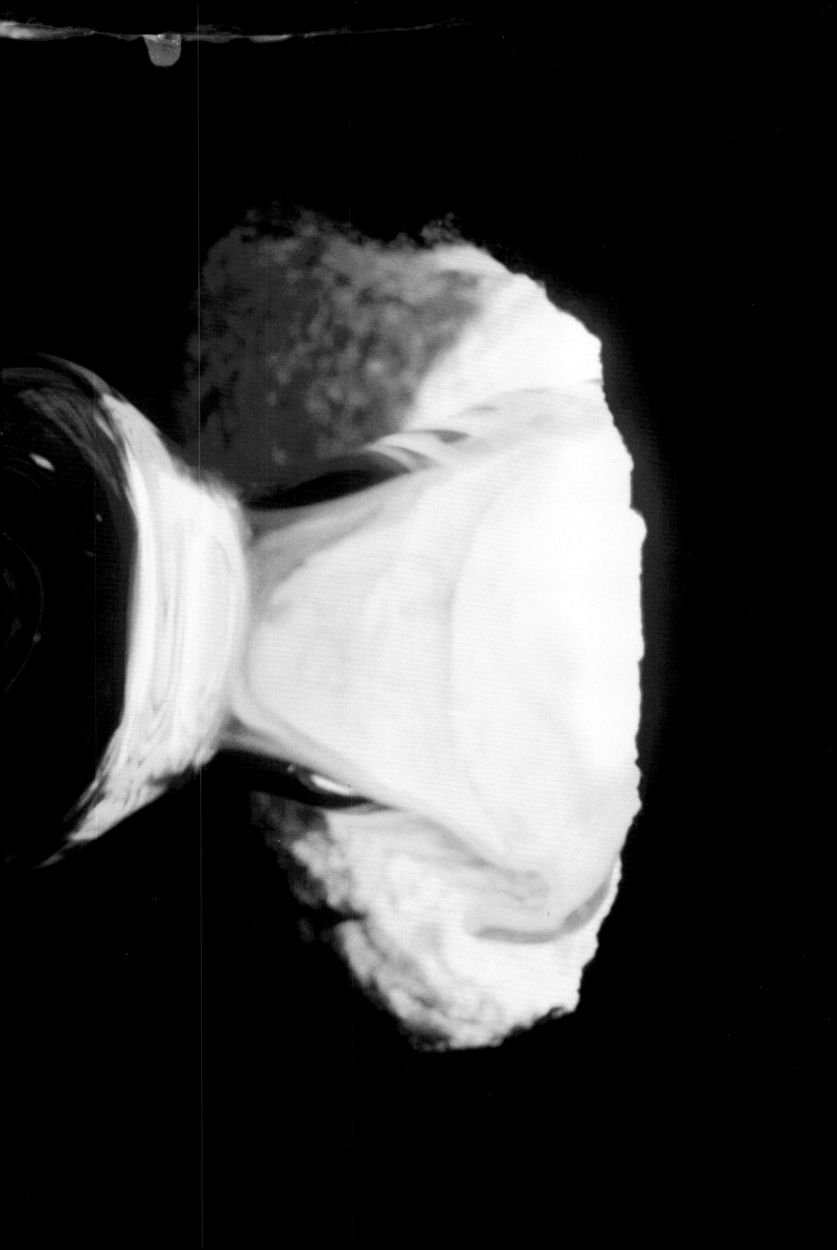

What distinguishes crystal from ordinary glass? The key is powdery red lead oxide—and it is Waterford's high lead content (approximately 33 percent) that produces its special sparkle. Other ingredients include ultra-white silica sand, which makes up almost half of the mixture, potash and a small amount of decoloring agents. They are mixed together and topped by bits of broken crystal (cullet) taken from earlier rejects. When fired, the cullet melts quickly, helping the raw materials fuse into a molten mass.

Thick-walled ceramic pots, approximately four feet high and three feet in diameter, sit on ledges inside the firebrick furnaces and are gradually heated from underneath by oil flame. Clay is used because it withstands high heat and imparts no color to the glass. The pots last about two weeks before being replaced.

The temperature inside the furnaces is brought to 1,200° C. In about 36 hours the ingredients reach the proper state of melting. A higher heat is used for stemware because of the flexibility required in forming, while the arm of a chandelier needs lower heat because its long, thin shape must cool quickly and set to avoid distortion.

Blowing: Most often the person putting the blow rod into the molten mass is the blower. There is little resistance to the rod as it is placed into the molten material. The blower gathers a 'lump' on the rod, rolling it to build-up the lump before pulling out the rod from the furnace. Rolling creates undesired ridges in the lump which must be smoothed away as soon as it is out of the furnace. This is done by the use of a hand-held wooden tool called a block.

The bulbous red-hot lump on the blowing rod immediately begins to cool and

solidify after leaving the furnace. It remains malleable (and quite hot) for several minutes, however, which is the time when all of the blowing and shaping must be completed. This requires skill, dexterity, and perfect timing on the part of each individual within the group. The team consists of a master blower, a qualified (journeyman would be the American equivalent) blower, and one or two apprentices.

At the same time that the blower is blowing, he is also turning the rod. This is vital for a smooth finish. The inside of the shaping forms are covered with burnt cork to help maintain smoothness and avoid ripples. After the newly-formed crystal piece is finished further processes follow.

If separate pieces must be added to the basic shape, handles, stems, tops, or bases, for example, a second rod is used to gather the molten lump. This one is solid because there is no blowing required. The molten crystal is shaped,

The art of blowing and the methods used today vary little from the olden days of 200 years ago. The hollow metal rod is much the same, as are the wooden shaping tools. These are made in the factory, from pearwood. They are boiled in water to saturate the wood as much as possible, thereby prolonging the tools' life, which is relatively short anyway because of the searing heat.

After the first rough shaping with a wooden block, a second, more precise block further pre-shapes the molten lump into its intended form. The blower then swings the lump-end of the rod into a wooden shaping form where the main blowing takes place.

Blowing requires strength and finesse. Since there is a tendency of hot air inside the molten mass to go up the blowing rod, the blower must counteract this while blowing into the molten material and creating the required cavity. Pressure must also be maintained until the molten crystal cools sufficiently to set.

then fused to the still-hot other part. A piece of stemware, for example, has three parts: the bowl, which is blown, and a stem and base (or foot), both of which are solid.

The tops of jugs are reheated in a small portable furnace known as a 'glory hole' to remelt the rims for shaping. The molten rims are actually cut with shears and then a cigar-sized steel rod is used to form the spout. The molten material for the handle is then quickly brought by an apprentice to the master for placement opposite the spout. As the handle cools, it is shaped into an arch with the steel rod.

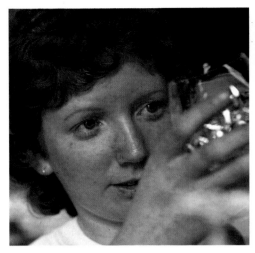

Annealing: The crystal pieces now leave the blowing area either by a conveyor system or are carried by hand. Because so many are fused sections, they must now be annealed. This is essentially a strengthening by uniform reheating. It is necessary because each piece or section cools separately and therefore contracts separately. Tapering also affects the time required to cool and contract. Thus, a stemware piece, for example, has its three parts each cooling at slightly different intervals. There is a danger, therefore, that they might come apart under routine stress. This is why the annealing oven is now used.

The annealing ovens are approximately 12 feet wide, 30 feet long and 6 feet high. A slow-moving conveyor belt rotates through the entire length of the oven. The crystal pieces are placed on the conveyor belt. As they pass through the oven, the pieces are gradually brought back up *near* to the melting point, and then gradually cooled down close to room temperature. The crystal is now firmly fused.

Inspection: Up until this point, inspection and rejection is done by the blowers themselves. At any time a flaw is noted or a mistake occurs, the unfinished crystal goes into the cullet box for remelting as raw material.

As the uncut crystal comes out of the annealing ovens, a separate team of inspectors must approve each piece. If a piece passes, the blowing team responsible for it is credited in a system that provides periodic pay bonuses dependent upon each team's successful output. If the crystal is rejected, team members are informed as to the reason so that mistakes are not repeated. Because of the high skill of the production teams, however, most of the crystal passes inspection.

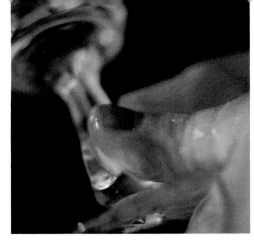

Diamond Cutting: Stemware and most bowls, at this point, are still spheres. They must now be cut to create surfaces at the top. This is referred to as 'cracking off the cap.' An industrial diamond is used to incise the cap but not cut it off entirely. The incised piece is then rotated in front of a flame which separates the cap from the rest of the piece. For thin rims, a diamond cannot be used to cut all the way through because it would cause chipping.

For large bowls at least 3/8" thick, such as vases and salad bowls, a diamond-tipped saw is used to remove the cap. They are then ground and polished to a uniform smoothness.

With stemware, a tungsten-carbide belt is used to smooth the rim and bevel the edges. The rims then go under a gas flame which melts away any sharpness. This is called glazing. The piece is then reannealed, as before, for uniform strength. The uncut crystal piece, called a blank, is now ready for cutting.

Cutting: All Waterford Crystal is cut. The cutting is done entirely by hand. Along with clarity and sparkle, cutting is a distinctive hallmark of Waterford

Crystal. Cutting patterns today are frequently based upon the original designs created during the era of the Penroses and the Gatchells during the 18th and 19th centuries. Today, with more than 700 cutters working for Waterford, it is the largest hand-cut crystal company in the world.

Basically, there are two types of cutting: wedge and flat. Wedge cutting is used for all of the intricate work. Waterford creates a relatively thick crystal blank so that deep cutting is possible. Deep wedge cutting creates prisms which diffuse light and intensify its reflection.

Flat cutting is broad and without detail but very slow and costly. It is an alternative to intricate wedge cutting that works in combination to offer contrast. Flat cutting also can reach areas of a piece which are otherwise inaccessible to the wedge cut.

Prior to cutting, the blanks are marked with felt-tip pens as a rough guide for the suite designs. But it is the cutter's own sight and feel which are the true guides to position and depth.

Cutters, like blowers, work in teams. They are usually in line along a bench of cutting wheels. The master cutter is at one end, followed by a qualified cutter and one or two apprentices. The wheels vary in diameter from 2 to 4 inches, depending upon the piece being cut.

All initial cuts are done by the master. He uses a carborundum wheel, holding the crystal blank over the top half of the wheel while resting his elbows on the bench. He is responsible for the most critical cuts, and then passes the piece along for finishing cuts by the other members of the team, who use fine sandstone wheels.

It is essential that uniformity be maintained and, when the design has panels, that they match up correctly. This often requires looking through the crystal. Narrow neck pieces, such as certain vases

and decanters, present special problems because it is hard to see clearly and accurately when the other side is so close.

Footed pieces, such as stemware, are difficult to cut around the bottom of their bowls because this area can only be reached at angles. Otherwise. the foot (base) will strike the cutting wheel. Water runs over the cutting surface so that the cutter can continually inspect his work. It also keeps the crystal cool, thereby avoiding the risk of cracking.

As with the blowers, the work of cutting teams is subject to separate inspection, and they also receive pay bonuses based upon output.

Engraving: Only a small amount of Waterford Crystal is engraved, primarily, trophies and limited edition pieces. Engraving is a difficult skill requiring great patience. Large pieces are especially difficult because the engraver must rest the piece on his fingertips. The heavier the piece, the more often the engraver must rest his fingers.

Like cutters, engravers use wheels for incision. But the wheels used by engravers are much smaller than those used by cutters. Engraving wheels range from 1mm to 2 inches in diameter. They are

usually made of copper, coated with a paste of carborundum powder and linseed oil. The paste, which does the actual grinding, is continuously applied to the wheel. The area on the crystal that is to be engraved has been left clear. The engraver draws his subject in outline, noting where the deepest grooves are to be made.

In a human figure, for example, areas such as the nose and eyes, would require the deepest cuts.

In engraving, the cutting is always below the surface and therefore the most pro-

minently-appearing elements go the furthest below the surface. This is the opposite of bas-relief work on pottery.

After the deep engraving is complete, the engraver lightly polishes that area for contrast. The general frosted appearance comes from the cutting effect of the paste.

Throughout the creation of a piece, the engraver must be careful about the effect of changing light as he turns the piece. Differing angles of light can give a false sense of depth. The engraver must, therefore, continuously return to his original point of examination to avoid distortion.

The Suites

Open Plain Diamonds

ILCASH

County Tipperary

Kilcash, a small town at the foot of the Slievenamon mountains, is in the center of a variety of romantic ruins, including Kilcash Castle. It is close to Carrick-On-Suir and this river marks the boundary between Tipperary and Waterford, a rewarding area for the fisherman and the sportsman.

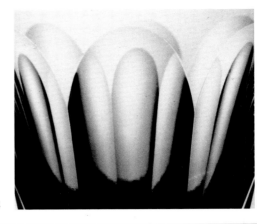

Flat Cuts

 **G**LENCREE

Glencree is a gentle, wooded valley which meanders with determination from somehere near Kippure mountain in County Wicklow almost to Enniskerry village. The valley where the waters of the Glencree and Dargle begin to mingle was once dark with the oak trees which were said to have been cut down for Eleanor of Acquitaine (1122-1204), wife of Henry II, who used them to roof her palace at Westminster. The Glencree Valley she regarded as her royal park.

To the east of the valley, at the foot of the mountains, there has been for many years vast, rugged stone buildings which were once a barracks built by the British army following the rising of 1798. They have since been used as a reformatory for boys, as a staging post for refugees from the communist takeover of Hungary and as settings for film making. Today they are the vigorous headquarters of the Glencree Peace and Reconciliation Center.

DUNMORE

The Big Fort

Dunmore is a very popular summer holiday seaside village on the Eastern side of Waterford harbor. It looks across the water to the famous Hook Head Lighthouse.

Fine Diamonds

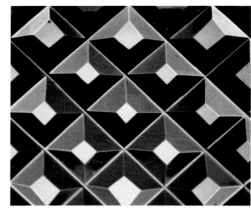

Open Plain Diamonds

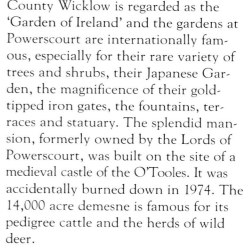

POWERSCOURT

County Wicklow is regarded as the 'Garden of Ireland' and the gardens at Powerscourt are internationally famous, especially for their rare variety of trees and shrubs, their Japanese Garden, the magnificence of their gold-tipped iron gates, the fountains, terraces and statuary. The splendid mansion, formerly owned by the Lords of Powerscourt, was built on the site of a medieval castle of the O'Tooles. It was accidentally burned down in 1974. The 14,000 acre demesne is famous for its pedigree cattle and the herds of wild deer.

The Powerscourt Waterfall which cascades sharply from a 40 feet high rocky crag, is the highest waterfall in the British Isles. It is open to the public all the year round. The demesne, restaurant, garden center, armory and shops are open during the summer. Only 12 miles south of Dublin, it is one of the city citizens' favorite outings. There are spectacular views of the Big and the Little Sugarloaf mountains from every part of the gardens which are approached by a long avenue of beech trees from the village of Enniskerry. Much of John Boorman's film "Excalibur" was made on the Powerscourt estate.

KENMARE

Ceann Mara—Head of the Sea

Kenmare is a small angling town at the head of Kenmare Bay in County Kerry, 21 miles south of Killarney. In this area there are a number of those mysterious megalithic stone circles. Reenagoppul Stone Circle is a shallow, chambered tomb at the center of 15 stones, its center covered by a massive, rounded capstone. Despite a certain lack of tidiness in the surroundings, it is a place of considerable atmosphere. Elsewhere around Kenmare there are a remarkable number of holy wells.

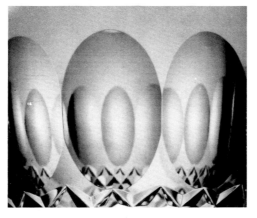

Olives

Open Plain Diamonds

COMERAGH

The Comeragh Mountains run south from Clonmel in County Tipperary and so down to County Waterford. The Nore Valley, named for the river which runs alongside the Comeraghs, is most picturesque. Here there are wooded slopes, lakes and streams, a favorite and well organized scenic area for the pony trekkers as well as the mountain climbers.

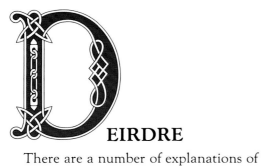 EIRDRE

There are a number of explanations of the meaning of this name. Some of the Gaelic language academics think it could mean "she who murmurs or chatters, or the raging one."

Mostly it is coupled with Deirdre of the Sorrows, the girl who met a tragic death when she eloped with her lover. The name Deirdre became popular at the beginning of this century with the revival of interest in all things Celtic. The poet W.B. Yeats made an ancient legend into a tragedy for his verse play, Three Sorrowful Tales of Erinn (1907), and a few years later, the dramatist, John Millington Synge made it into a verse drama, Deirdre of the Sorrows.

Wedge Cuts

GALTEE

The Galtee Mountains in County Tipperary have an attractive assembly point for climbers at Cahir (Cathair Dhuin Iascaigh—Fortress of the Dun Abounding in Fish). Apart from the good fishing from the adjacent rivers Suir and Aherlow, Cahir also has a Castle. It is of the 15th Century and was built on the site of an earlier fortress built by the great warrior, Brian Boru. Cahir Castle surpasses in size all other castles of its period in Ireland and it has lately been restored and is open for guided tours during the summer. It has endured a long and embattled history and owes its comparatively unscathed survival to the fact that its guardian surrendered it to Cromwell without a shot being fired.

From Cahir the road runs prettily through the Glen of Aherlow at the foot of the Galtees to the town of Tipperary. This is rich dairying country, famed for its cheese and bacon.

Flat Cuts

ROSSMORE

The Big Promontory

Rossmore Park, a mile or so out of Monaghan, formerly a large family estate belonging to the Barons of Rossmore of the Westenra family, has now been divided between the Government Forest and Wildlife Service, the local golf club and a housing estate.

In the neighborhood is the beautifully timbered estate of Glaslough House. Although Monaghan is a comparatively small, land-locked county, there is Lough Emy which is remarkable for the extraordinary number of wild fowl and swans which inhabit the lake.

Plain Diamonds

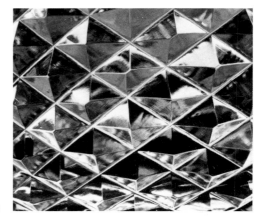

Plain Diamonds

ALANA

Alana is a girl's name though it is seldom used nowadays. Where the English would say 'darling,' the Irish would probably say 'Alana.'

TRAMORE

Tra More—The Great Beach

Tramore, eight miles along the coast from Waterford, heads the list of favorite Irish holiday places.

Blaze (perpendicular)

KINSALE

Ceann Saile—Tide Head

Kinsale is on the Bandon River in County Cork, the biggest county in Ireland. Kinsale still remembers the siege of 1601 when the Spanish took it over and held it against the English army for a year. The Irish, under the Earls of Tyrone and Tyrconnell, marched down from the north, joined by the local chieftains, to join the Spanish. But the following year the superior English army broke the siege and defeated both the Spanish and the Irish in one of the most decisive battles in Irish history. Afterwards no Irish were permitted to live inside Kinsale walls and it became the chief port of the British navy until the passing of the sailing ships.

William Penn, founder of the State of Pennsylvania was Clerk to the Admiralty Court in Kinsale and his father, Admiral Penn was governor of the town.

Today Kinsale is one of the most popular yachting harbors on the south coast—it has a sailing school—and is one of the best equipped for sea angling. It has a Good Food Circle and there is a Kinsale Gourmet Festival every October and a Regatta during the summer sailing season.

Open Plain Diamonds

Open Plain Diamonds

TYRONE

Tyrone is an inland county with access to the waters of Ireland's biggest lake, Lough Neagh. Dungannon on the southern shore of the lake is a big marketing and industrial center, especially for the linen industry. In medieval times it was the headquarters of the princely O'Neills. In 1646 the Irish army, led by Owen Roe O'Neill had one of its all too rare victories when it defeated the English and Scottish forces led by General Munro.

In the 18th and 19th centuries Tyrone had many connections with America. It was John Dunlap, formerly of Strabane, who founded the *Pennsylvania Packet* in 1771 and it was he who printed the Declaration of Independence. The grandfather of President Woodrow Wilson, also a Strabane printer, emigrated to the U.S.A. in 1807.

The River Blackwater in Tyrone has salmon, trout, pike, perch and bream, and golf and greyhound racing keep the sportsmen busy. Tyrone is one of the six counties of Northern Ireland.

Blaze (unequal)

AUREEN

In Irish Maire, which is an obvious borrowing from Mary. Its popularity as a girls' name has been comparatively recent because, together with most people in Western Europe, the god-fearing Irish would not presume to call their daughters after Jesus's mother. In Ireland Maire, another form of Maureen, is one of the more usual forms of the original Mary.

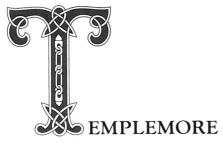

TEMPLEMORE

The Big Church

The North Tipperary Foxhounds hunt the district around Templemore on the River Suir, also famed for its good fishing. How the Devil's Bit Mountain (1,577 feet) got its name is legendary. It seems that when the Devil had taken his bite and not finding it to his liking, he spat it out onto the plain below, thus forming the Rock of Cashel.

Plain Diamonds

DONEGAL

Dun na Gall—The Fortress of the Foreigners

The foreigners referred to in the Irish version of this town in the northwest came from a hundred miles up the road, a telling demonstration of the insularity of pre-medieval days.

Donegal town was the seat of the O'Donnells, princes of Tyrconnell and the remains of their castle on the bank of the River Eske is very impressive.

An important literary work was written in the nearby Franciscan abbey. This valuable historical record known as The Annals of the Four Masters, was written by the monks.

Donegal County has a wealth of historic ruins and references. In Donegal Bay the fishing fleet returning with its catch to Killybegs escorted by hungry sea birds is a lively sight. It is a deeply indented coastline, full of little bays and high forelands. While inland, it is an ever-changing panorama of deep gorges, high mountains and deep lakes.

Donegal people are remarkably industrious and for generations they have been foremost in the hand weaving of tweeds and the embroidering of fine linen which is also decorated with intricate crochet work.

Rosette

Steps

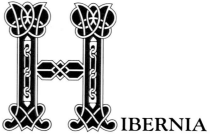

HIBERNIA

Roman and Greek writers called
Ireland Hibernia. The Romans knew
about Ireland from reports they got
from traders along its coasts. The
Romans never invaded Ireland
although it is said that Agricola
thought of it but was forbidden by his
Roman government.

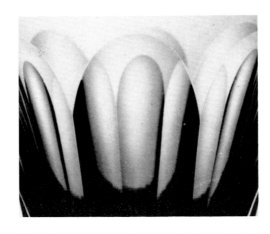

Flat Cuts

CURRAGHMORE

About 10 miles south of the city of Waterford, Curraghmore is the seat of the Marquis of Waterford. It is a vast demesne set in beautiful country by the River Clodagh. The gardens are open to the public, but not the mansion.

KERRY

The most vociferous of all Irish counties, the jokes about the sayings of the Kerrymen are a part of the humor of Ireland. The full force of the Atlantic has given this southwestern county its great beaches. In contrast the hinterland rises dramatically into peaks and mountains dominated by Macgillycuddy's Reeks.

The Iveragh Peninsula provides the famous Ring of Kerry drive through the little fishing villages; Kenmare, Sneem, Waterville, Cahirciveen, Glenbeigh and on to Killorglin and southwest to the famed Killarney of lakes: salmon and trout fishing and golf and international seminars at its many big hotels by the lake.

Caherdaniel, also on the Ring, is the birthplace of "The Liberator," Daniel O'Connell (1775-1847) who mastermined Catholic emancipation, which was granted to Ireland in 1829 after over a hundred years of religious oppression.

The Dingle Peninsula is 30 miles long. Its chief town, Dingle is a great place for catching and eating good fish. In the old Spanish trading days it was the chief port of Kerry. Further out along the peninsula there is an Irish-speaking district.

Wedge Cuts

SHEILA

In Irish it is Síle, which springs from the Latin Caecilia and, like so many other personal names, it came to Ireland with the Anglo-Normans.

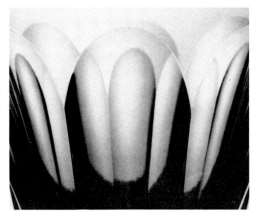

Flat Cuts

Facets

TRALEE

Traigh Li—Beach of the River Lee

Tralee, the chief town of County Kerry, is the focal point of Tralee Bay and is also the gateway to the lovely Dingle peninsula where there are enough superb scenic drives to keep the motorist happy for a week.

In medieval times it was the seat of the Desmond family, a branch of the Anglo-Norman FitzGeralds. Thirteen of their earls are buried in the old Dominican cemetery.

Every autumn there is great merriment in the town when pretty girls who can claim a drop of Irish blood arrive from all over the world for the festival whose highlight is the choosing of the Rose of Tralee, inspired by the popular song written in the 19th Century and immortalized by Count John McCormack, Ireland's greatest operatic and concert tenor.

From Fenit, at the tip of Tralee Bay, Kerry's patron saint, Brendan the Navigator (484-577) is said to have sailed across the Atlantic to the New World of America. A few years ago, to prove it was possible, Tim Severin and his crew succeeded in making the hazardous voyage from Fenit to Newfoundland in a reconstruction of Saint Brendan's leather boat.

EILEEN

In a variety of forms ranging from
Evelyn to Emeline, this universally
popular name came to Ireland via the
Normans who, in turn, inherited it
from Old German. It was for many
generations a popular name with the
Norman Irish ladies. It was an Irish
Eileen who composed one of the most
poignant laments of the death in battle
of her husband, Art O'Leary. It was an
Eileen who inspired the ancient and
most beautiful of Irish love poems,
"Eileen Aroon."

Blaze (unequal)

Rosette

CLARE

The County of Clare in the west of Ireland is bordered on the south by the River Shannon. On the west its rugged coast peaks to the Cliffs of Moher rising 700 feet above sea level. The almost lunar landscape of the Burren is famous for its rare wild flowers.

Shannon International Airport is beside the estuary of Ireland's mightiest river. Along the road toward the ancient city of Limerick medieval banquets are held all the year round at Bunratty Castle, built long ago by the O'Briens of Thomond. This castle, which was restored most carefully in 1960, is furnished exactly as it would have been when it was a fortress in the 15th and 16th centuries.

Today the castle is surrounded by the peaceful setting of a folk park which includes a series of traditional local farmhouses, fishermens' and laborers' cottages and a forge. A few miles away is Cratloe Castle built in 1610 by the MacNamaras. The woods of Cratloe are said to have provided some of the oak which made the roof not only of Westminster Hall in London but also what is now the royal palace in Amsterdam.

Near Ennis, the capital of County Clare, is the ruins of the once magnificent Franciscan Quin Abbey which was built by the MacNamaras in 1402. There is also Knappogue Castle, restored by an American architect, which warms to the merriment of a nightly medieval banquet during the summer. Craggaunowen Castle has a different attraction, a museum and a reconstruction of a Bronze Age crannog or lake dwelling.

Wedge Cuts

KILDARE
Cill Dara—the Church of the Oak

The lush, flat grassland of Kildare is the focal point for the important Irish horse breeding industry. At the National Stud at Tully, horses are bred and trained to compete in all the international shows, including the annual Dublin Horse Show.

The Curragh, Kildare, is a vast acreage of unfenced grass cropped by hundreds of sheep wandering across the road which cuts through it from Newbridge to Kildare town. Since earliest times it has been the headquarters of Irish racing and for the Irish Derby and many other classics. In the same area is Naas with its famous race course and, three miles away, Punchestown, the great steeple-chasing challenge.

For more than a century the Curragh Camp has been an important military establishment and here the Irish army does much of its training.

The Dukes of Leinster, once the premier dukedom of Ireland, of the ubiquitous Fitzgerald family, had their country mansion at Carton House, in County Kildare, a magnificent palace with landscaped gardens around lakes which made a very beautiful background for much of the film "Barry Lyndon."

Wedge Cuts

KYLEMORE

The Pass of Kylemore and its three lakes are all popular angling waters deep in Connemara country in the County of Galway. The impressive castellated Abbey of Kylemore perched above the lake was built by a wealthy businessman in the 19th century. When his daughter fell from her horse and was killed the family went away.

Earlier in this century the Abbey became a refuge for an order of nuns from Belgium. For many years it has been a girls' school run by the Irish Benedictine Dames.

Connemara is a region like no other in Ireland—a land of grey stone walls, high, bare mountains, blue, blue sea, dark lakes, turf cutting for fuel and sturdy, cream-colored Connemara ponies. The strange, stark grandeur of this part of County Galway has been the inspiration of many painters. These are the remains of once splendid castles, most of them ruined, several of them restored and occupied, mostly by Americans. Along the sea coast a new form of Irish enterprise is bringing life and a measure of prosperity. The building of 'traditional' Irish thatched cottages, enhanced by modern conveniences, was begun some years ago. Owned and run by a local co-operative, they are popular with Irish families on holidays as much as by visitors from abroad.

KATHLEEN

Kathleen Mavourneen, Kathleen ni Houlihan, are two of the many poetic names given to Ireland. This Irish girl's name which came to Ireland with the Normans originated with the virgin martyr Catherine of Alexandria, a 4th century saint revered by the Crusaders. Her name became popular in Ireland in the middle ages and continues so to the present day.

Flat Cuts

CASTLETOWN

Close to the village of Celbridge in County Kildare, the Palladian style mansion of Castletown reigns supreme. It was built in 1722 for William Connolly, the Speaker of the Irish House of Commons and designed by the Italian architect Alessandro Galilei. The interior is decorated with magnificent plasterwork.

It was bought, and continues to be magnificently restored and maintained, by the very active Irish Georgian Society. All year round in the exotic long gallery painted in the Pompeian manner there are recitals, receptions, seminars, lectures and balls. In June when the series of concerts in Irish country houses are held, Castletown is host to top international musical celebrities.

During the Winter the Honourable Desmond Guinness, President of the Society is one of a number of specialist lecturers who tour the United States of America, speaking about the house and attracting interested Americans to make gifts of much needed finance and furnishings. There are very active branches of the Irish Georgian Society in London and in various parts of America.

The river Liffey flows past Castletown and nearby Celbridge Abbey where Esther Vanhomrigh, Jonathan Swift's (1667-1745) ill-fated 'Vanessa,' lived. Here the Gloomy Dean often came from Dublin to visit her.

The Honourable Desmond Guinness, who owned Castletown, has given it over to The Castletown Foundation, which is a non-profit educational trust which came into being in 1979.

Rings

Plain Diamonds

CASHEL

Caiseal Mumhan
The Stone Fort of Munster

A small town, a crossroads with a famous monument. The Rock is a spectacular sight presiding over the surrounding area. Here, 200 feet above the plain the kings of Munster had their seat from 370 AD to 1101 AD when King Murtagh O'Brien handed it over to the church. It was on this Rock of Cashel in 450 A.D. that St. Patrick baptised King Aengus and his family. Here, too, Brian Boru, who was to defeat the Danes at the battle of Clontarf, was crowned King of Munster.

Cormac's chapel, built in the 12th century, is one of the gems of local ecclesiastical architecture. Here also are the remains of the huge cathedral and a massive castle. There is a perfect round tower 92 feet high. Below in the town the former palace of the archbishops has been conveniently transformed into a hotel.

Wedge Cuts

ROSSLARE

Ros Lair—The Middle Peninsula

Rosslare is a popular seaside resort, 11 miles south from Wexford town. It is a long curve of golden beach which stretches for six miles and is safe for bathing at all states of the tide.

Rosslare Harbor, just 100 miles from the capital city of Dublin, is the terminus for the car ferries which sail throughout the year between Fishguard in Wales and Le Havre in France, a very busy service during the summer season.

Out to sea the light from the ancient Tuskar Rock lighthouse can be seen for 19 miles. The weatherman who gives the forecasts on the radio uses Carnsore Point, the extreme tip of the County Wexford coast, as one of his daily references.

In this area, too, at Ballysampson, Tacumshane, is the birthplace of Commander John Cary, 'father' of the American navy. He is commemorated by a fine statue looking out to sea in Wexford town.

Wedge Cuts

GLENGARRIFF

The Rugged Glen

Glengarriff in County Cork is a tourist mecca. A small inlet high up into Bantry Bay, it is so sheltered that many trees and shrubs and flowers native to the Mediterranean flourish there. Glengarriff Harbor is dotted with numerous small, heavily wooded islands. Ilnacullin, or Garinish Island, was landscaped very successfully many years ago to resemble an Italian garden. Now the property of the nation, it is much visited by the admiring public.

NNISFAIL

Inis—Island Fail—Destiny

Innisfail is yet another poetic name for Ireland. The Lia (stone) fail is an Irish legend which stems from the stone on which Jacob is reported in the Bible as having been asleep on when he dreamed of the heavenly ladder.

It is believed that the Liafail came with one of Ireland's earliest colonists, the Dedannans, who used it at Tara in County Meath as the inauguration stone of the kings.

When Tara fell from power it was transferred to Scotland where the Liafail became the coronation stone of the kings of Scotland—the famous Stone of Scone.

In the 13th century Edward I of England brought it to London where it has been used at Westminster Abbey as the coronation stone.

144

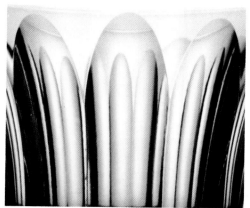

Flutes

COLLEEN

Colleen is an Irish word for a young girl. Although it has been much used in popular song and drama—"The Colleen Bawn" by Dion Boucicault, for instance, it is now seldom used as a first name in Ireland but remains popular abroad, particularly in America.

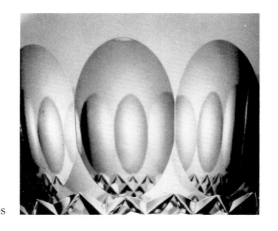

Olives

Blaze (perpendicular)

BLARNEY

An Bhlarna—The Plain

In the County of Cork the village of
Blarney is famous for its castle with the
Blarney Stone which is supposed to
confer eloquence on those who succeed
in kissing it. How it came by its name
sounds authentic enough. Cormac
MacDermot MacCarthy, Lord of
Blarney Castle, was requested by
Queen Elizabeth's representative in
Ireland to renounce his Irish chief-
taincy and acknowledge the tenure of
his lands as from the Crown. In a
regular stream of letters he appeared to
be about to agree, but kept putting off
the actual decision until the enraged
Elizabeth, seeing through his fair
words and soft speech, declared "This
is all Blarney." And so Blarney passed
into the English language to describe
pleasant talk intended to deceive
without offending.

 ISMORE

Lios Mor Mochuda
Mochuda's Great Enclosure

Lismore is the most historic town in the County of Waterford. In Ireland's golden age in the 7th and 8th centuries it was a university center. Lismore Castle, perched spectacularly on a cliff high above the River Blackwater, has passed through many owners, endured many wars and pillages. It was once the seat of the archbishops. From Sir Walter Raleigh it passed to the Earl of Cork and it has been in the possession of the Dukes of Devonshire for centuries.

The village has many interesting ecclessiastical ruins and the fishing in the Blackwater can be very worthwhile.

Wedge Cuts

DUNLOE

The Gap of Dunloe in County Kerry is a rocky gorge that runs for four miles between the Macgillicuddy's Reeks and the Purple Mountains. It is one of the most popular tourist trails in all of "Killarney's lakes and fells." To negotiate it the visitor must take ponies for the trek to enjoy the view of Dunloe Castle, and the terrifyingly massive rocks on either side of the streams tumbling from the myraids of lakes. An added attraction is the echoes which are given back eerily by the close formation of the rocks and the hills.

The Gap is 795 feet above sea level, descending gradually to the Lakes of Killarney. There is a change from foot, or pony, to boat so that the journey can be concluded with the thrill of shooting rapids.

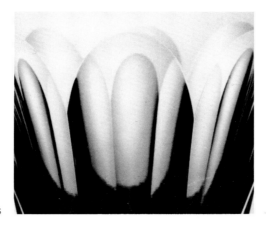

Flat Cuts

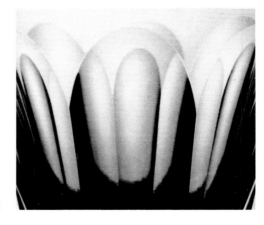

Flat Cuts

ROYAL TARA

In pagan times Tara, six miles south of Navan in County Meath, was the political, religious and cultural capital of Ireland. Here, every three years on this low mound there was a feis, a national assembly, where laws were passed, tribal disputes were settled and the strategies of peace and war were discussed. Here, too, kings were enthroned and by the end of the session the king who was crowned in the palace at Tara was the most powerful of all the five kingdoms of Ireland. Thomas Moore (1779-1852), whose Irish melodies arranged from traditional airs took London by storm in early Victorian days, wrote some very poignant verses around this historic gathering place; "The harp that once through Tara's Halls" and "When Malachy wore the collar of gold." Malachy II, who died in 1022, was the last of the High Kings to enjoy the glories of Tara, which waned with the spread of Christianity. Little remains now of the once great banqueting hall erected by Cormac MacAirt, the third century High King, to accommodate the crown princes, chieftains, priests, poets, musicians and officials who assembled there every three years for the great feis.

GLENMORE

Glenmore means the big glen and there are many of them among the Irish foothills. This one refers to the small town a few miles north of Waterford but actually in the County of Kilkenny.

Rings

ASHLING

Ashling is an ancient girl's name meaning "dream of beauty", and is also a very pretty little town in County Waterford.

Ball Cuts

Open Plain Diamonds

BOYNE

The Valley of the River Boyne is one of the most historic areas in all Ireland. On its banks at Bonore in July 1690 William III defeated the exile James II for the crown of England. The Irish who were on the losing Jacobite side suffered a terrible defeat.

At Slane on a hill high above the plain of County Meath, in A.D. 443 St. Patrick lit the Pascal fire which brought the light of Christianity to Ireland. But long, long before that there was New Grange, regarded by most archaeologists today as the most ancient, fascinating and mysterious of all the ancient burial places in the western world. This legendary place of kings who came to Ireland in 4000 B.C.—from where, no one knows—has been faithfully reconstructed and is open to visitors. Much archaeological excavation remains to be done on the nearby neolithic tumuli at nearby Knowth and Dowth where even more interesting finds may yet be discovered.

The Boyne valley is well endowed with ancient castles, one of the best survivors is at Slane, seat of the Conyngham family where there are mementoes of George IV, including a magnificent circular ballroom/library completed for his visit in 1821 during the height of his liaison with the Marchioness of Conyngham.

Navan is the county town where the Boyne and Blackwater rivers meet and the Meath Foxhounds and the Tara Harriers hunt the area.

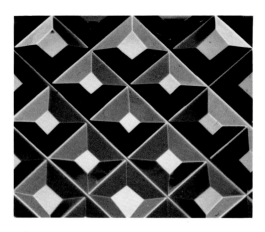

Open Plain Diamonds

 **DARE**

Ath Dara—The Ford of the Oak Tree

Adare, in County Limerick, is a model village of quaint, thatch roofed cottages and gardens tumbling with flowers. Salmon and trout live in the river Maigue. Overlooking that fertile river the Franciscan Friary founded by the Earl of Kildare in 1464 has long since fallen into graceful but preserved ruin.

The 13th century Trinitarian Abbey had the distinction of being the only place in Ireland for the redemption of Christian captives during the Third Crusade. The 14th century Augustinian Abbey was possibly another of the Earl of Kildare's creations. These FitzGerald Earls of Kildare had their strongly fortified Desmond castle at Adare for almost 400 years until Cromwell had it dismantled in 1657.

Later the estate was bought by Thady Quin, ancestor of the Earls of Dunraven who, in the 19th century, built the neo-Gothic Adare Manor —one of Ireland's stately homes open to the public during the summer.

MOURNE

The Mourne Mountains in County Down on the east coast are almost half way between Belfast in Northern Ireland and Dublin in the Republic. For fifteen miles they range from Rostrevor on Carlingford Lough to Newcastle where Slieve Donard rises almost 3000 feet above the sea.

This is excellent walking and climbing country and the views from the top of the peaks are very rewarding. On clear days the view from the top of Slieve Donard encompasses Donegal in the north west to Wicklow in the south east and over the sea to Scotland and the Isle of Man.

It was Percy French (1884-1920) who made the Mournes world famous with his charming song, "Where the Mountains of Mourne Sweep Down to the Sea."

At the base of the Mournes there is said to be one of the three "waves" of ancient Irish legend. When their mighty roar can be distinguished it was said to forewarn the death of a chieftain.

Blaze (unequal)

Shapes &
Patterns

	Goblet	Champagne	Champ. Saucer
Adare Eileen Galtee Tramore			
Alana Ashling Clare Lismore			
Boyne Cashel Colleen Donegal Kathleen Kilcash Maureen			
Castletown Curraghmore Powerscourt			
Glenmore Sheila Templemore Tyrone			
Innisfail Royal Tara			
Glencree Kenmare Kinsale Kylemore Rosslare			
Comeragh Glengarriff Kildare			

BARWARE

	12 oz. D/Old Fash.	12oz. Hi Ball	14 oz. Ice tea
Alana Colleen Lismore Kylemore			

White Wine	Hock	Cocktail	Port	Sherry	Cordial	12 oz. Tumbler	9 oz. Old Fash.
Claret	Hock	Cocktail	Port	Sherry	Cordial	12 oz. Tumbler	9 oz. Old Fash.
Claret	Hock	Cocktail	Port	Sherry	Cordial	12 oz. Tumbler	9 oz. Old Fash.
Claret	Hock	Cocktail	Port	Sherry	Cordial	12 oz. Tumbler	9 oz. Old Fash.
Claret	Hock	Cocktail	Port	Sherry	Cordial	12 oz. Tumbler	9 oz. Old Fash.
Claret		Cocktail	Port	Sherry	Cordial	12 oz. Tumbler	9 oz. Old Fash.
Claret	Hock	Cocktail	Port	Sherry	Cordial	12 oz. Tumbler	9 oz. Old Fash.
Claret	Hock	Cocktail	Port	Sherry	Cordial	12 oz. Tumbler	9 oz. Old Fash.
12 oz. Brandy	Oversize Wine						

Town &
County

he pageant of Irish history is preserved in the narrow lanes and streets of Waterford which criss-cross uphill from the broad River Suir. From many nations ships voyage up through Waterford's wide harbor to berth alongside the city's quays as they have been doing since the first invaders came to Ireland. This was long before history was recorded, other than in the archaeologist's delight of megalithic tombs, dolmens, graves etc., dating back to 2000 B.C., which are spread around the city's circumference.

Today the container lorries packed with Waterford crystal travel the main road north to the port of Dublin from where the delicate crystal cargo is airfreighted, or loaded onto the cargo ships on the River Liffey. When the Penroses set up their glass factory in Waterford in 1783 the availability of the sea route for their export trade was one of the bonuses.

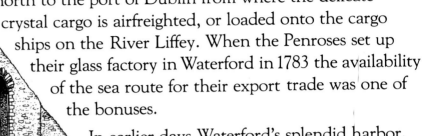

Grey Friar's Abbey, also known as the French Church, built c. 1240.

In earlier days Waterford's splendid harbor, far from being a bonus, was the main focus of the invading forces who have both riven and enriched the Irish race. The first recorded people were the Celts. In Ireland, the Irish tribe which settled around the Waterford area became known as the Decies or D'eise. They had two ruling families, the O'Faolains (Anglicised to Whelan) and the O'Brics. All that is left of that name is *Ballybricken Green* where bull baiting used to be held.

Toward the end of the eighth century the fierce Viking sea robbers from the cold, dark Icelandic waters began to sail up the River Suir in their long boats, to settle on its lush river banks to enjoy its equable climate. Vikings, Norsemen, Danes, Swedes, Finns—we call them all Scandinavians now—gave the name Vadrefjord, Weatherford, to Waterford. Like the warrior Celts, they too believed that the only way to happiness in the next life was through a hero's death in battle. Fortunately they had also a practical side. They were not only the originators of the cities of Wexford and Waterford, but also of the capital, Dublin. To the Irish who were a nomadic people, preferring cattle dealing to tillage, they introduced the idea of towns and the intricacies of commerce.

Naturally, the Celtic Decies and the Viking Danes had many battles though, sometimes they might join forces and go raiding abroad to Britain or Scotland.

For over 300 years, from the strategic harbors of Wexford and Waterford, the Vikings controlled Ireland's south east coast. In 1003, Raynvald, son of the Norse king, Sigtrygg, is credited with the building of *Reginald's Tower*, Waterford's proudest architectural monument. When the much reviled Dermot MacMurroough was deposed as King of Leinster, he went across to Britain to recruit help in his ambition to unite all Ireland with himself as High King. He offered his nubile daughter, Aoife, a battered bride if ever there was one, as bait to Strongbow, Earl of Pembroke, to encourage him and his Norman armies to come to his aid. It was in Reginald's Tower that he held the celebrations of the nuptials and while the rude revelry went on inside, outside the Celts and Vikings were vainly battling with the Normans. Daniel MacLise was so inspired by the episode he painted a horrific picture of the carnage on one of the biggest canvases now in the National Gallery in Dublin.

The English kings came in the wake of the conquering Normans and it was in Reginald's Tower that Henry II (1154-1189) held court; King John (1199-1216) set up a mint for Irish coinage; Richard II (1377-1399)

stayed during his Royal visit. It was from Reginald's Tower that King James II (1685-1688), fleeing from his defeat at the battle of the Boyne, waved farewell to Ireland before he sailed to exile in France.

Reginald's Tower is a civic museum now, housing a magnificent collection of charters bestowed on the city by a variety of English monarchs, together with their militaria, all in excellent condition.

Gradually the Irish, the Celts and the Norsemen merged into a Christian community. Then, in 1169, came the Normans, men of great military strength and formidable discipline. They engulfed Ireland but, eventually, they were to enrich it too, with their talent for integration, their leadership and their architecture. They spread out all over the country, building castles and churches.

The English who came with the Anglo-Norman invasion, although they also helped themselves to thousands of fertile Irish acres, for the most part kept aloof from the local people, behaving as colonists rather than settlers.

As the Pope in faraway Rome tried, not always successfully, to govern the Irish church, so the kings of England insisted on loyalty from what George Bernard Shaw centuries later described as 'John Bull's Other Island'. In fact, at one period the church in Ireland had gone so considerably off the Roman rails that the Pope sent King Henry II (1154-1189) to see if he could curb its many abuses. The same Henry II was so pleased with Waterford he dubbed it a royal city.

In 1487, following the Wars of the Roses, Henry VII was having difficulty keeping his throne from his many rivals. Within a space of ten years two most unqualified claimants attempted to usurp his throne. First the notorious Perkin Warbeck, followed by Lambert Simnel accompanied by a huge army of supporters. Dublin crowned Warbeck, much to the fury of Henry II. Simnel, who arrived via Cork was also enthusiastically received, but Royal Waterford repulsed Simnel and his traitors with bloody deeds on both sides. For this loyalty Henry conferred on the city the title 'Urbs Intacta Manet

Waterford'—'the unconquered city of Waterford' which the city's coat of arms bears to this present day.

It was Elizabeth I in 1574 who caused Waterford city to become a County, separate from the surrounding counties, particularly Kilkenny and Tipperary which were not so favorably disposed towards her.

The dreaded Oliver Cromwell camped at the gates of Waterford in the winter of 1648. He found the resistance so strong and the weather so severe he eventually went back to England sending his son-in-law Ireton's army to burst open the gates and capture the city in the summer.

Second only to Dublin in importance as an Anglo-Norman port and stronghold, Waterford, with its loyalty to the English monarchy, was, in fact, largely influenced by the English tradition right down to the last century. Its peculiar individuality is reflected in the history of its many churches. Henry VIII's turbulent church reformation was resisted strongly in Waterford, the majortiy of whose citizens adhered to the Old Faith.

Four early 18th century houses on the Mall, which is one of the most graceful streets in Waterford.

Christ Church Cathedral was founded in 1050 by the Christian Viking, Reginald who also built the enduring tower of the same name. The Anglo-Normans improved the church's architecture. In Henry VIII's reign its altars were demolished and its property confiscated. General Ireton's soldiers later used it as a barracks and melted down the church treasures. In 1793 it was rebuilt to the designs of Waterford's prolific architect, John Roberts. Today, although it needs extensive repairs, it is regarded as the finest 18th century church in Ireland.

John Roberts, a Protestant and great grandfather of the Victorian Field Marshall Lord Roberts of Kandahar, also designed the *Catholic Cathedral*. Much strife between the Christian churches had to be endured before that was finally achieved. In 1690, when the Irish armies had been beaten at the Battle of the Boyne, Waterford's four Catholic churches had been forced to close. Catholic worship was a very clandestine undertaking but they beavered away for more than a century until they triumphantly built the Cathedral of the Holy Trinity in 1796. To celebrate its recent renovation Waterford Crystal donated a magnificent set of chandeliers.

Ruined churches and abbeys are jostled by the rising tide of commercial buildings in Waterford's narrow streets. The French Church, or *Grey Friar's Abbey*, recalls the Cromwellian times when there was an effort to boost the Protestant population by establishing a colony of French Calvinists, or Huguenots. They were to replace the Catholics who Cromwell had banished to Connaught or sent as slaves to the sugar plantations of Jamaica, encouraged by Admiral William Penn.

Waterford is an easy city to walk about. Every place of significance can be found easily on a small map. Remnants of the old city walls and defence towers built by the Danes and Anglo-Normans are still standing. The Quays which turn right at Reginald's tower to become The Mall are the most important thoroughfares. In The Mall the City Hall, though in need of a good tidying, is an elegant 18th century building boasting a magnificent old Waterford crystal chandelier, a replica of which was sent to the Independence Hall of Philadelphia in 1802. The full dinner service of old Waterford crystal in the Council Chamber was presented by Senator Edward Maguire whose family came from the city. Thomas Francis Meagher (1823-1867), was born in what is now the Granville Hotel on the Quay. He was sentenced to death for his part in the 1848 Young Ireland Rising but he escaped to America where he fought in the Civil War. His Brigadier General's uniform, swords and the battle flag of the Irish Brigade he carried at Fredricksburg, is displayed on the walls of the chamber.

The *Theatre Royal*, also part of the City Hall, is constantly used for plays and for the annual Waterford Light Opera festival. Waterford was the birthplace of William Wallace (1814-1865), composer of 'Maritana' and other operas which were very popular with the biggest

Modern Waterford chandeliers in the Oak Room, Fitzgerald's, the Munster Bar, Waterford.

audiences he could command in England and abroad. Coincidentally he was born in the same house in Colebeck Street as another man of the world, the eminent actor, Charles John Keane (1811-1868).

A remarkable number of eminent ecclesiastics were born in Waterford. Father Luke Wadding (1588-1657), historian, philosopher and linguist, was president of the Irish College at Salamanca and founder of the Irish College of Saint Isodore in Rome. Four Jesuit brothers, all cousins of his, were distinguished for their scholarship in the ecclesiastical centers of Europe.

The Christian brothers were the inspiration of Edmund Ignatius Rice, a Waterford man who channeled his vocation and his wealth into founding the schools which have educated so many of Ireland's prominent men since 1762.

In the mid 18th century the gentry who had money and many who had not, vied with each other in the splendor of the town and country houses they commissioned from leading architects. Waterford was prosperous and Waterford was fortunate to have John Roberts to design most of its important church and civic buildings. The city divides itself into quarters, mostly no bigger than streets. Ballybricken was the venue for the cruel medieval sport of bull-baiting and cockfighting. Similar to any Irish town or city, Waterford is not lacking in pubs and people to fill them. The difference is that many of the lush, modern Waterford ones make a feature of their crystal lightingware. In the Munster Bar upstairs the antique wood-paneled room which used to be a part of the Marquess of Waterford's town house makes a rare and historically interesting lounge bar.

Reginald's Tower, built in 1003 by the Danes against attack by the Celts.

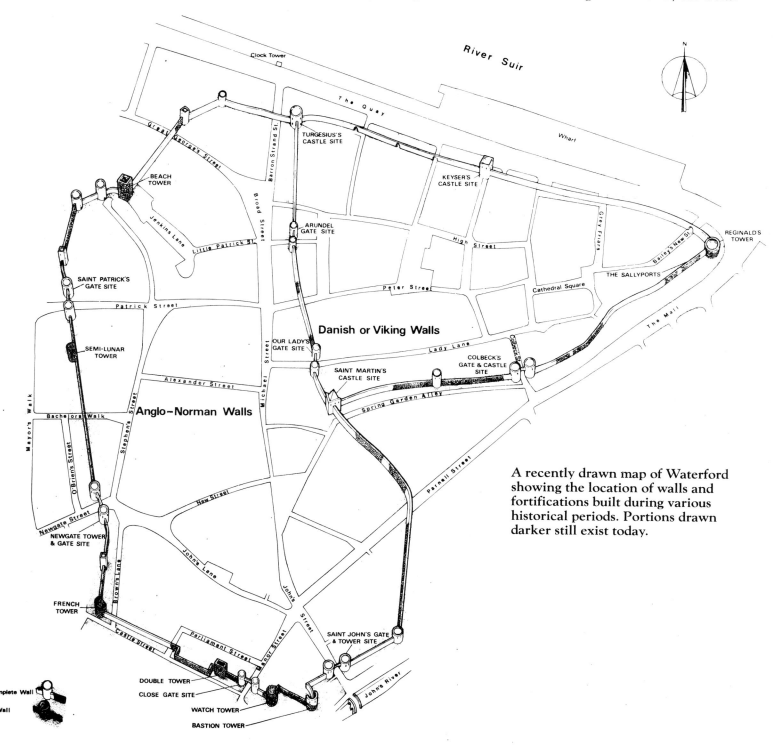

A recently drawn map of Waterford showing the location of walls and fortifications built during various historical periods. Portions drawn darker still exist today.

175

The Chamber of Commerce, once the Morris family home, is a splendid example of Georgian architecture. The Art Gallery, which has a good collection of contemporary Irish paintings, and the Municipal Library, are housed in another former family house. *The Quays* are Waterford's jugular vein. From here the traffic flowed out to Europe, America, England; salt, fish, fabrics, corn, whisky and meat. Wine came up the Suir from France and Spain. Today the meat factories are closing down while the cattle goes on the hoof, shipped to the Middle East. When the ships were provisioned here for the long voyage to America many young Waterford men went with them to Newfoundland and it was they and their families who founded the city of St. John's, named from their home parish.

To reach Waterford from the north or west all traffic must come across the wide Suir over the Redmond Bridge. It supplanted the old "Timbertoes" bridge which was built in 1797 by Samuel Cox, a Boston architect.

The Allied Irish Bank Building was built early in this century on the site of Turgesius' Tower, a massive Viking fortress which formed part of the city's riverside defenses.

Waterford County

The River Suir and the *Knockmealdown* mountains enclose County Waterford on the north. To the south a coastline indented with bays and headlands or stretched out into sandy beaches begins with Dunmore East at Waterford Harbor reaching out as far as Youghal across the Blackwater River in County Cork. The fertile land supports beef, tillage, corn, sugar beet, dairying. The River Blackwater is one of the best salmon rivers, in fact the county is networked by rivers which yield trout, chad, roach. Dungarvan, the adminstrative center for the county, with the Comeragh and Monavullagh mountains as the backdrop, is the focal point for deep sea angling. The four work bays of the Waterford Crystal factory are only across the road from the sea.

This, too, is hunting country for the West Waterford Foxhounds and the Dungarvan Harriers. It is an historic area where, in the third century, the Decies tribe originally from Meath, came to lord it over

the rest of the populace. The destruction of the ancient church and castle were, as usual, by discourtesy of the Cromwellians. It was McGrath country once and across the bridge over the Coligan River in Abbeyside is the remains of the 12th century McGrath castle. Not too many miles away, outstanding at a road junction is a memorial to the most celebrated of the name "Master McGrath," a greyhound who won the Waterloo Cup three times between 1868 and '71 and was beaten but once in the thirty-seven courses he ran in public.

Mount Melleray Abbey, a modern Trappist monastery was founded in 1833 by monks whose Cistercian order had originally been driven from France. Sir Richard Keane, a wealthy Cappoquin lawyer, gave them 600 acres of barren moorland which, together with donations from generous wills (and their own skills) they eventually turned into a self-supporting farm with a complex of impressive stone buildings. For the past few years these silent monks have been restoring their church. There is spartan accommodation for any man or woman who wants relief from this materialist world. There are no fixed charges but honorariums are acceptable.

Lismore

In the 17th and 18th centuries the 'big houses' came to be a most important feature of the Irish countryside. Mostly they were built by the Anglo Irish, many of them men and women of culture who had traveled abroad and were anxious to bring some of their enlightenment to the countryside at their gates. Like the monks of earlier days they knew a good site when they saw it, which is why so many of the stately homes of Ireland, and England too, are built atop the ruins of former monasteries.

The typical example is *Lismore Castle* built high up on a tree-faced precipice which drops vertiginously down to the River Blackwater. In the Dark Ages of Europe when Ireland was reputed to be the land of saints and scholars, Lismore, in the eighth century, had a university renowned in Europe presided over by Saint Colman. It was to be savaged by the Danes and finally destroyed by the Norman Raymond le Gros in 1173.

Henry II built a castle on the ruins where he received the submission of the Irish chieftains. In Elizabethan times 'adventurers' and younger sons were sent to Ireland where her administrators could arrange grants of land for them. Sir Walter Raleigh got Lismore Castle, but preferred Youghal and sold it to another adventurer, Richard, the great Earl of Cork, one of whose many sons was Richard Boyle, the chemist who originated Boyle's Law. James II stayed a night at Lismore Castle, almost overcome when he looked down from the drawing room window at the river far below.

A Boyle heiress brought it into the Cavendish family, the Devonshires, who entertained Lady Caroline Lamb when her family brought her there to try to make her forget Byron. The sixth Duke of Devonshire, the Bachelor Duke, is responsible for the elaborate castellated building which survives. His friend, gardener and handyman developed into Sir Joseph Paxton, his architect and designer in 1851 of the Crystal Palace. During the renovations of 1814 the Lismore Crozier and the Book of Lismore, hidden by the monks long, long ago, were discovered, adding to the treasures of Ireland and the National Museum.

Lismore was the favorite home of the late Adele Astaire, the actress-dancer sister of Fred Astaire who married a Cavendish. The short, narrow, stony avenue leading to the castle is neatly clothed in dark green velvet moss from the stones on the roadway and the walls to the trunks of the trees, so damp is this valley of the Blackwater. Today's most renowned Lismore inhabitant is Dervla Murphy, the travel writer who cycled around India on her bicycle and writes with affection of her native Lismore. All the country in the Blackwater valley is beautiful, but to take the steep road out of the town and follow the "Vee" road through the Knockmealdowns into Mitchelstown is to have the most spectacular view of neighboring Tipperary County.

A nice example of trying, and failing, to keep up with the neighbors in 1808 is on the roadside at Ballysaggartmore, not too far from

Lismore, where the Kellys built themselves the most extravagant gothic entrance gates but ran out of money before they could build the house to match them.

Blackwater Mansions

The winding Blackwater and its fish-filled tributaries was a most fashionable area for the builders of impressive mansions. At *Ballynatray*, built in 1795 on the site of a ruined abbey, they have marked the tomb of Raymond le Gros, Strongbow's companion in invasion and the builder of the splendid Hook House lighthouse on the Wexford Harbor which is still very much in use. On the opposite side of the harbor mouth is Crook Head which gave rise to the saying among those who sailed between them in time of war that they got to Waterford 'By Hook or by Crook.'

Branches of the Norman-Irish FitzGeralds and their castles, not by all means ruined, are all over south west Ireland. Above the Blackwater at Knockanane, Strancally Castle has used the ruins of an old Desmond castle as foundations—the FitzGeralds were Earls of Desmond.

Below: Village of Ballyhack, just above Waterford Harbor on River Suir, viewed from Passage East. Right: The fishing village of Passage East. Lower right: A quiet scene in the Comaragh Mountains outside Waterford.

Curraghmore

Another continuing Norman Irish family are the Le Poers, or
Powers. One of their seats, a Tudor Baronial gem is Gurteen-le-Poer,
at Kilsheelan on the River Suir near the mountains of Slievenaman,
the subject of one of the poet Thomas Moore's sad melodies.

The most magnificent house in the whole county is Curraghmore
which has been in the De Le Poer family since they crossed over the
seas to Ireland in the 12th century. At one time, lacking a son and
heir, Lady Catherine Power the heiress married Sir Marcus Beresford
and so, now they are the Le Poer Beresfords, Marquises of
Waterford, whose various forebears have created this distinctive
house like no other in Ireland. Inside there are wall and ceiling
paintings by Johann Vanderhagen. The redecoration done in 1780
by James Wyatt remains enchanting. The vast forecourt which
encloses a range of stables was designed by the ubiquitous John
Roberts of Waterford. The Saint Hubert stag with genuine antlers
holding a crucifix, the crest of the De La Poers, sits aloft on the high
tower over the main door built over the ancient castle. The gardens

were possibly inspired by Versailles. The public is allowed to visit the Shell House put together in 1750 by Catherine, Countess of Tyrone, whose white marble statue by Van Nost shimmers eerily in the dim, damp light. Much of the 2600 acres estate is thickly wooded and families of pheasants can impede the motorist on the long avenue. Horsemanship continues to be an important pursuit at Curraghmore. Lord Marcus Beresford was responsible for the racing stables of those two very diverse monarchs, Edward VII and George V.

Riding schools abound in Ireland, everywhere, but the Whitfield Polo School at Kilmedda, not far from Curraghmore on the Waterford road must surely be unique.

Dromana

The Blackwater passes through a handsomely wooded valley at the market town of Cappoquin four miles from Dromana. This was once the castle of the FitzGeralds who adopted the ancient Irish title of Lords of the Decies, the name of the surrounding area. The family is still in Dromana, a splendid Georgian manor perched on the rubble of the old castle on a rocky plateau rising high above a broad stretch of the Blackwater. The view across this expanse of water to the Knockmealdowns and the Galtees, the greens, and golds, and the silver of the woods in the ever changing light so peculiar to the Irish countryside, is an enchantment which must have been enjoyed by generations who have lived there.

There was no law against female inheritance and through the marriages of various daughters in ensuing generations the FitzGerald patronymic was metamorphosized to Villiers Stuart with a few Barons and Earls of Grandison in between. At one time the Villiers Stuarts were extremely rich. Following the English fashion, they built a most commodious house complete with a ballroom, beside the earlier one. Around 1780, one of the family, the second Earl of Grandison, built this quite palatial house with splendid furnishings.

View from Cheekpoint, where the rivers Nore, Barrow, and Suir meet and flow on to become Waterford Harbor a few miles below.

Although the Villiers Stuarts had long since changed the Old Faith for Protestantism, Henry Villiers Stuart put himself up as candidate for the Catholics in the famous County Waterford election of 1826. His surprising victory over Lord George Beresford of Curraghmore opened the way for the Catholic Emancipation Act of 1829.

Not far from the house, Villierstown, is an attractive village, the conception of what used to be known as 'improving landlords.' One of the Earls of Grandison brought weavers from Ulster where the linen industry was flourishing and set them to weaving. He built them a model village and did everything to ensure they would not be diverted from their work by having to farm. But, like the glass industry of the time it was not to last for very long.

In 1957 most of the estate was sold to the Department of Lands. A cousin and his wife, Mr. and Mrs. FitzGerald Villiers Stuart, bought the remaining land and demolished the grand house, reverting to the original Georgian manor. The former long avenue to the house, now a public road where trees planted by the Forestry Commission are growing steadily, crosses the tiny Finiska River by a fanciful bridge through a Hindu Gothic arch complete with minarets, spires and fretted windows. This oriental folly was built to welcome home a newly wed Villiers Stuart and his Viennese bride who were so charmed with it they had it rebuilt in more enduring materials. As time went by it began to decay so badly that the Irish Georgian Society took it under their wing and, in 1968, completed its repair with all their usual thoroughness.

Some Poets

The County of Waterford is by no means all stately homes and hunting, shooting and fishing. For instance, from a cluster of villages in the Kilmacthomas area west of Waterford City once lived the roistering schoolmaster poet, Donnchadh Ruadh Mac Conmara. Not every scholar believes he got to Newfoundland but the poem he wrote about an emigrant voyage, "The Adventures of a Luckless Fellow", is a classic. He earned his living mostly school teaching and traveling, but always writing in Irish. "The Fair Hills of Ireland" *(Ban Chnoisc Eire ann Oigh)*, is one of his best remembered and most nostalgic poems. He was known all over Ireland from his wanderings.

Tadgh Gaelach O Suilleabhain, about the same time, lived in Kilmacthomas, and more recently, Riobard Weldon, who died in 1914, is regarded as the poet of the Decies district.

Irish Speaking Areas

Tramore, seven miles south of Waterford, is traditionally the leading Irish family resort. It has long sandy beaches, an 18 hole golf course, an Irish Disneyland of entertainment for children, plus boating, sea-angling and dancing, without which no Irish village would be complete.

The General Post Office was built on Custom House Quay in 1876.

Further west, along the coast, Waterford can boast of having the first modern college of Irish. It was founded in 1835 by a pioneer of the language revival, and well ahead of the Gaelic League. There are still districts in the county where Irish is the first language in the home.

Ardmore, on the southernmost tip of County Waterford, is more than another stretch of sandy beach ruffled by the Atlantic. It has the most perfect round tower in Ireland. It is 97 feet high, fifteen feet in circumference and not a stone out of place. It was the watch tower for the seventh century monastic settlement founded by St. Declan.

Whether by sea or by land, the monks could see the approach of any potential enemy. If necessary, they could clamber up into the doorway and pull up the high ladder, cutting themselves off from attack. With the arrival of Cromwell and his gunpowder this tactic was no longer effective. Miraculously, St. Declan's beautifully symmetrical tower has survived all the invaders. St. Declan's Holy Well still draws the devout and on the beach, St. Declan's boulder, poised on two rocks, is said to cure or prevent backache for those who can manage to crawl under it.

Here, even before the monks, lived the chieftain of the Decies, or, in Irish, D'eise. Below the steep hilly village of Ardmore the smooth sandy beach where people love to bathe when summers are kindly, can be very volatile. It gets some of the Atlantic's gale force winds and in winter storms many ships have been wrecked here, even as recently as 1947 when an ill-equipped coal boat bound from Wales was wrecked and the crew died from exposure in the boats.

The novelist and playwright, M. J. Farrell (she also writes in her own name, Molly Keane), lives in a house perched high above the beach. She turns a saturnine pen to the single-minded pursuit of the horse and hunting by the people of the big houses who have all too often not the necessary finance.

In summer small boats cruise up and down the Suir and its sister river, the Barrow in County Wexford. Gourmet dinners by candlelight are provided abroad by some of these well-equipped crusiers. Such relaxed living was not always available on these waters. Celts, Vikings, Normans and Cromwellians as well as civilian steam boats, or yachts aiming for Waterford have all first to pass through the hazards of getting into Waterford Harbor.

Close by the same fishing village of Crook is Dunmore East (the Big Fort). Dunmore East was a fashionable watering place in the 19th century and still is, especially for yachting people and deep sea anglers. The Gulf Stream warms these southernmost waters of Ireland and from Dungarvan to Hook Head there is great game every year when the Blue Shark appears in the Atlantic. Cod, ling, conger, tope, skate, and dogfish are all around to tempt the fisherman to the chase and provide the locals with a summer living, supplying the boats and the gear.

The houses at Dunmmore East rise in tiers up from the harbor, among them some authentic Irish thatched cottages. This is one of the seaside places where the Irishman and his family from generation to generation have come for their summer holidays.

From Dunmore East to Waterford the road passes through pleasant pastoral country, past Woodtown where Jacqueline Kennedy and her children spent a quiet, recuperative holiday when she was first widowed.

Towards the end of the 18th century the Irish parliament gave a grant of £50,000 to a group of gold and silversmiths to come from Geneva to form a colony of crafts workers on a site overlooking the harbor. It did not long survive and the building was turned into a British military barracks which is why the ruins have long since been known as the Geneva Barracks.

Seven miles short of Waterford, the quiet little Village of Passage East overlooking the sea was once a fortress commanding the passage of all the ships coming or going up and down the River Suir. Lacking an Eiffel Tower or a Rockefeller Center, the best panoramic view of the city of Waterford is from Cheekpoint Hill. It is a modest hill, but from the top there is a view of Waterford's many spires, its boundary and life line, the River Suir and the distant mountain ranges.

Descending from the hill and entering the narrow streets of the city center, a visitor on foot soon gets a feel for Waterford. There is nothing particularly precious about it; the old mixes with the new with great abandon. Still, it exudes its own charm, this quiet river port that holds so much Irish history within its ancient walls. It is fitting, then, for a visitor to depart the city via the road to Cork, stopping at the outskirts in the neighborhood of Kilbarry for a tour of the company as well known as its home. That they share the name of Waterford is most appropriate: Waterford and crystal, two words inseparable to so many.

The Quay and Reginald's Tower.

Limited Editions & Master Cutter Pieces

Limited Editions

In 1971, a series of annual limited edition vases was introduced. They appear on pages 197-207. Each of the vases is approximately 11 inches high and four inches wide. Each vase is cut and engraved. Like cutting and blowing this is all done by hand. Copper-wheel engraving is, however, particularly time consuming and, therefore, editions have been limited to 250 pieces each year.

The series began with engraved religious themes. They are: 1971—The Magi; 1972—The Ten Commandments; 1973—Noah; 1974—Prodigal Son; 1975—Samson, and 1976—King David. In 1977, the themes switched to Shakespearean subjects. They are: 1977—Macbeth; 1978—Hamlet; 1979—Julius Caesar; 1980—Falstaff, and 1981—Richard III.

Master Cutter Pieces

The title of master is earned by the craftsman, who has successfully completed eight years of training, including a five year apprenticeship and a three year period as a qualified cutter.

Each of the pieces in this collection is one-of-a-kind. Apart from the normal production, a master may elect to cut a design of his own idea on an existing blank of crystal, typically a large bowl or vase. This is a project undertaken on his own time, and serves as a creative break and design exercise away from regular production.

As is evident to anyone who has ever visited the Waterford factory, these men take great pride in their work. A Master Cutter's Piece, therefore, is a representation of the cutting skill and artistry that the person has accumulated over many years of endeavor.

Six examples of Master Cutter's Pieces are shown in this chapter. The total number of these unique pieces created each year is quite small. This fact, plus their inherent beauty, is the reason for their great appeal among collectors.

Master Cutter Piece

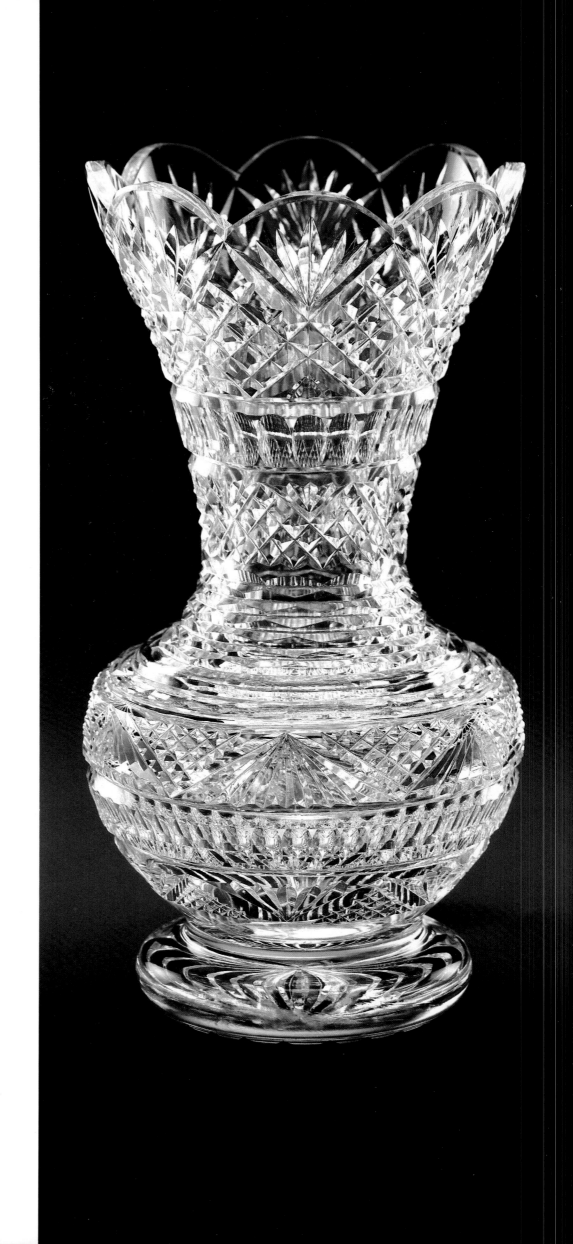

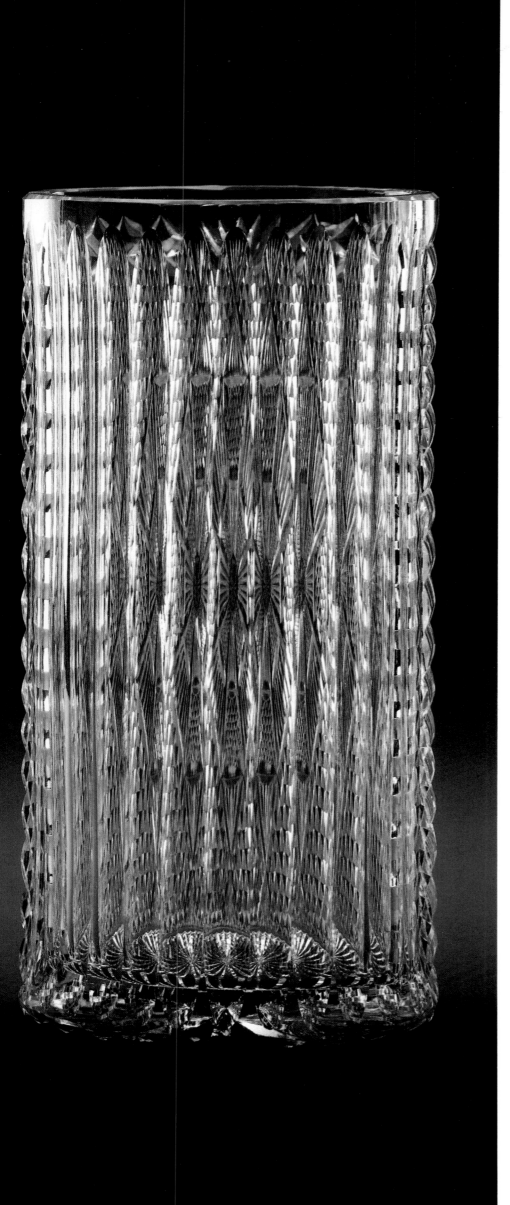

Master Cutter Pieces left and right

Master Cutter pieces left and right

Master Cutter Piece

**Limited Edition
1971—The Magi**

Limited Edition
1972—Ten Commandments

Limited Edition
1973—Noah

Limited Edition
1974—Prodigal Son

**Limited Edition
1975—Samson**

Limited Edition
1976—King David

Macbeth

**Limited Edition
1977—Macbeth**

Limited Edition
1978—Hamlet

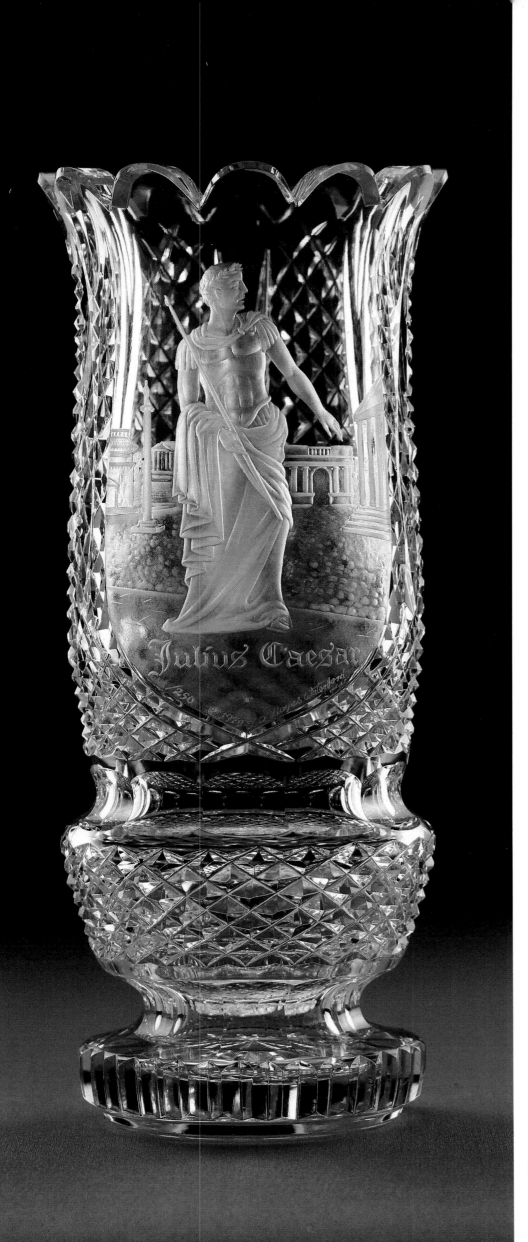

Limited Edition
1979—Julius Caesar

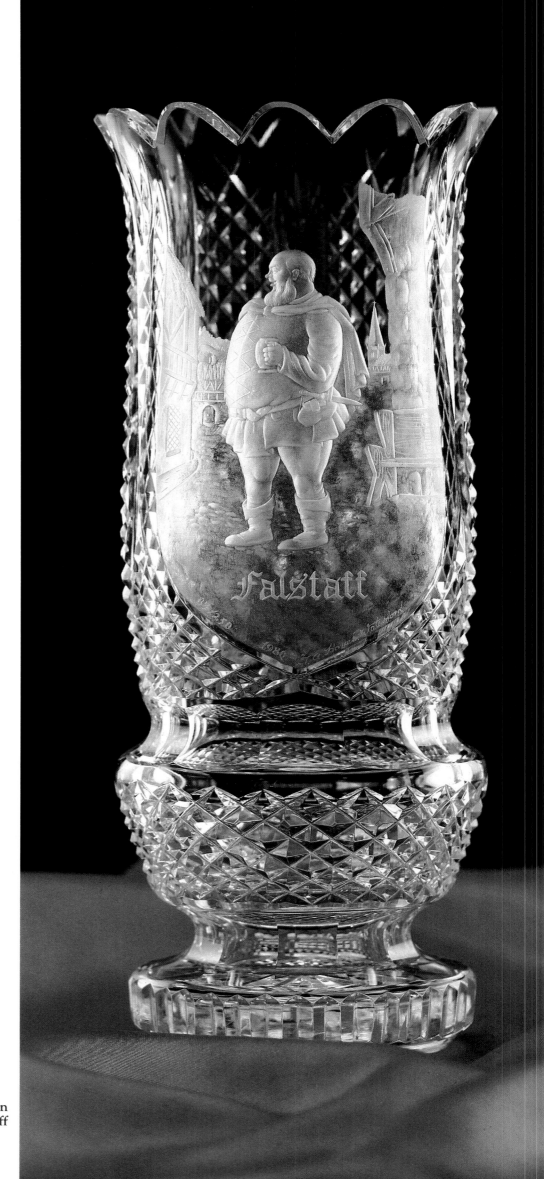

Limited Edition
1980—Falstaff

Limited Edition
1981—Richard III

Still Lifes

A selection of Waterford vases picked for the variety of shapes, cuts and sizes that are available.

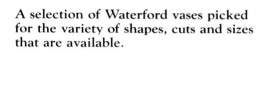

1

2

3

4

5

6

7

11

8

12

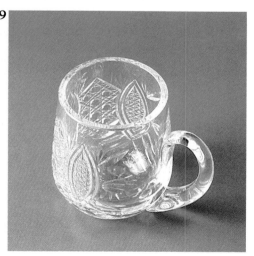

9

Six-sided Ashtray (1), Cigarette holder (2), Ashtrays (3, 4, 5), Tobacco jar (6), Ashtrays (7, 8), Mugs (9, 10), Cigarette holder (11), Ashtray (12).

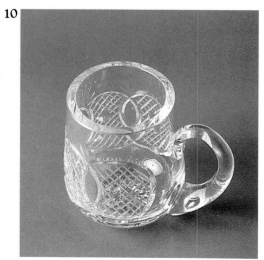

10

1

2

3

4

5

6

7

8

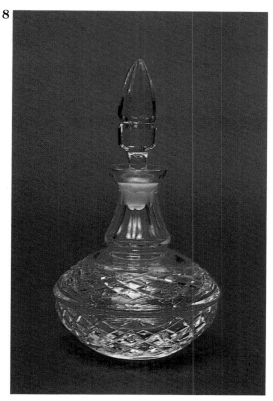

9

Candlestick (1), Lustre (2), Candle-
sticks (3, 4, 5). Vanity collection:
Powder box, Ring holder, Scent bottle
(6), Mini Hurricane (7), Scent bottle (8),
Powder box (9).

1

2

3

7

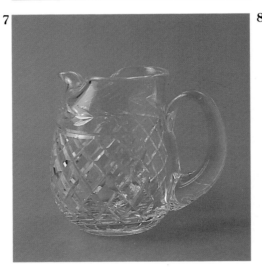

8

11

4

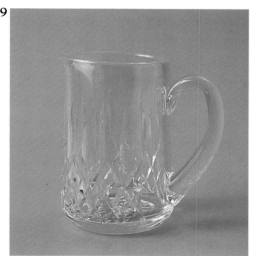

5

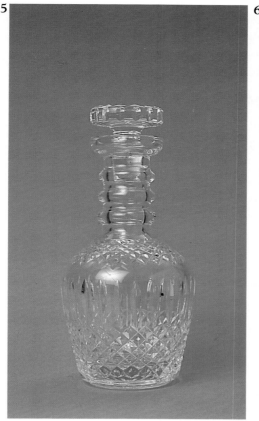

6

9

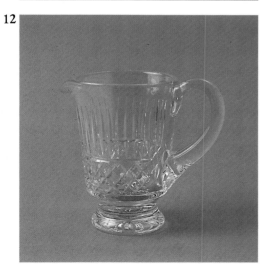

10

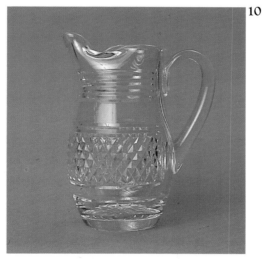

12

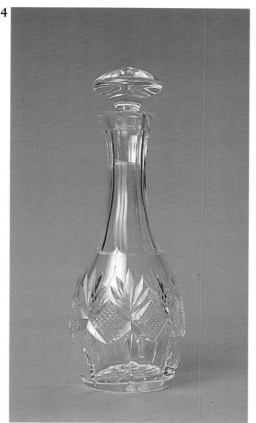

Decanters and Jugs: Three-ring spirit decanter (1), spirit decanter (2), square spirit decanter (3), liqueur decanter (4), three-ring decanter (5), ship's decanter (6), ice lip jug (7), Royal Tara jug (8), Lismore jug (9), Martini pitcher (10), Colleen jug (11), and Tramore jug (12).

Above and opposite: a selection of
bowls, demonstrating the wide variety
of sizes, shapes and styles available.

Footed sugar and creamer (1), Sugar and creamer (2), Compote (3), Cake stand (4), Footed salt and pepper (5), Marmalade jar (6), Salt and pepper (7), Rose bowl (8), Celery tray (9), The crystal slipper (10), Crystal tray (11), Crystal tiara (12), Lismore biscuit barrel (13), Cowboy boot (14).

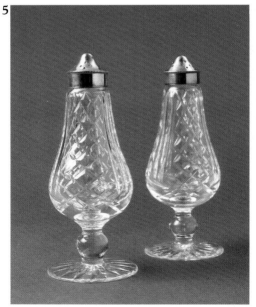

Contemporary lighting ware by
Waterford. Fabric shades are silk and
silk blends, bases and fittings are brass.

Architectural Studies

This pretty oval room used to be used as a billiard room during the 18th and 19th centuries. It is known as the Wedgwood Room on account of the style of its decoration—pale blue walls and white circular plaques in the manner made famous by the English Wedgwood factory.

Architecture

What characterizes Waterford and epitomizes its essential nature is a connection with the past. Out of its history burgeons inestimable contributions to the art of interior design.

One way to judge the power of the presence of Waterford in a room might be to consider the effect of its absence.

Examine the photographs in this section. Mentally subtract the Waterford and try to visualize the rooms.

The effect is devastating.

It is undeniable that Waterford chandeliers make their presence felt, whether in the most historic of environments (Westminster Abbey) or in contemporary places (Kennedy Center).

In any objective critique of decor, it would generally be acknowledged that Waterford transmits a sense of character, style, history, identity to an area, and pulls it all into focus.

Above: Waterford Cathedral—with special Waterford chandeliers.

Right: Old Waterford candelabra in Council Chamber, Waterford.

Opposite: The Mayor of Waterford, Alderman Tom Brennan in Council Chamber, City Hall, Waterford.

Shelbourne Hotel, Dublin

The Shelbourne Hotel was started by Martin Burke from Co. Tipperary in 1824 on the north side of St. Stephen's Green. With the move of the Duke of Leinster to Leinster House (now Dail Eireann—the Irish Parliament) just off St. Stephen's Green from the north side of the city the area had become one of the most fashionable in the city. Built to look like four town houses the hotel was first known as Burke's Hotel and later became the Shelbourne, named after William, second Earl of Shelbourne whose family had strong connections with St. Stephen's Green. The Waterford chandelier hangs in the entrance hall to the hotel.

Old Waterford chandelier in Gresham Hotel, Dublin.

Dublin Castle, The State Apartments Drawing Room

The State Apartments in Dublin Castle date mainly from the 18th century and were designed as a residence for the Lord Lieutenant of Ireland. They were also to be used for State occasions. During the 1914-18 World War the apartments were used as a Red Cross hospital and, after the burning of the Irish Courts building, the Four Courts, in 1922 they were used as the headquarters for the Courts for about eight years. The apartments are used regularly for State receptions and for ceremonies connected with the inauguration of the President of Ireland. The State Apartments are open to the public. The State Drawing Room was restored during the 1950's following an accidental fire in 1941 and was refurnished in 18th century French style. Badly damaged furniture was faithfully restored and copied. The chandeliers were installed during the restoration purchased from the newly-opened Waterford Glass factory.

Prime Minister (Taoiseach) of Ireland's Home

Abbeville, the home of Mr. Charles J. Haughey, T.D., Prime Minister (Taoiseach) of Ireland in June 1981, is an attractive house built on the outskirts of Dublin in the late 18th century for the Rt. Hon. John Beresford, Taster of the Wines in the Port of Dublin, brother of the first Marquess of Waterford, who was one of the most powerful men in Ireland. It is called Abbeville after a town in northern France from which Beresford's wife came. The Waterford chandelier, which hangs in the dining room, was installed 12 years ago by Mr. Haughey.

John F. Kennedy Center for the Performing Arts, Washington D.C.

The fabulous Waterford chandelier and wall sconces that hang in the South Lounge. They were a 1963 gift from the people of Ireland. The chandelier is eight feet across and weighs over 1,000 pounds. There are 4,000 individual pieces of crystal lighted with 116 bulbs.

Johnstown Castle, County Wexford

Johnstown Castle was built in the 13th century by the Anglo-Norman Esmonde family. It was presented to the nation in 1944 and is used as an agricultural college. It is situated in beautiful grounds which may be visited. The Waterford chandelier is located in the entrance hall of the castle.

Bank of Ireland (Old Parliament House), Dublin

The first stone of the new Irish Parliament House was laid in 1729 across the road from Trinity College, Dublin. The architect was the Surveyor-General of Ireland, Sir Edward Lovett-Pearce, of whose interiors the House of Lords (now the Court of Proprietors of the Bank) is the principal survivor. Several other architects, including James Gandon and Francis Johnston, built on additions to Lovett-Pearce's design. After the Act of Union, when the Irish Parliament was united with the Westminster Parliament, the building was purchased in 1804 by the Bank of Ireland for £40,000 ($80,000). The House of Lords is much as it was when the Lords ceased to use it and the great chandelier hanging there dates from the late 18th century and is thought to be either Waterford or Belgian. It is believed that it is one of a pair that hung originally in Parliament House.

Mansion House, Dublin

The Lord Mayor's residence, since 1715 the Mansion House, was built in 1705 by Joshua Dawson, after whom Dawson Street, where the house is located, is named. It has been the scene of many important events in Ireland, including the adoption of the Declaration of Independence in 1919 and the signing of the truce that ended Anglo-Irish hostilities in 1921. The Waterford Chandelier is located in the Oak Room.

National Museum of Ireland, Dublin

The Ceramics Room of the National Museum of Ireland is the final resting place for a very fine antique Waterford chandelier. Most of the chandelier is late 18th century with some early 19th century additions. There are very few known examples of early Waterford chandeliers as perfect as this one which was acquired by the museum from a private house.

The Royal Hibernian Hotel, Dublin

The Royal Hibernian Hotel is the oldest hotel in Dublin. It opened its doors in 1757 in Dawson Street where it still functions as one of Dublin's premier hotels. In the early 19th century the Royal Mail Coach Office and passengers embarked and disembarked outside the hotel on journeys all over Ireland. In 1960 the Lafayette Dining Room was completely refurbished and a Waterford chandelier, especially designed for the room, was installed.

Westminster Abbey, London

Ambassador Cinema, Dublin

Built in 1775 as the Assembly Rooms and known as the Rotunda because of the lofty, high hall, 80 feet in diameter which lay inside, the building adjoins the Rotunda Hospital (the first maternity hospital in Ireland or Great Britain) and was desgined by Richard Castle who designed so many other famous buildings in Ireland. Behind the Assembly Rooms were elegant gardens where bands played. Both the rooms and the gardens were popular with fashionable 18th century Dubliners. The income earned from these places went to the Rotunda Hospital which was run as a charity for expectant mothers. Today the Ambassador Cinema is housed in the Assembly Rooms, the lobby of which is lit by an elegant Waterford chandelier.

St. Paul's Chapel, New York City

Four of the 14 chandeliers in this Trinity Parish Church. They are probably Waterford and are believed to date to 1802.

At Home

Waterford lighting can also enhance contemporary decor, as this beautifully
decorated home in a suburb of New
York City shows.

City Hall, Dublin, Members Room

The City Hall, formerly the Royal Exchange, was started in 1768 from designs by the London architect Thomas Cooley and was completed in 1779 at a cost of £40,000 ($80,000), raised through lotteries. Adjoining Dublin Castle, City Hall stands on the site of Damer Gate, the eastern entrance to the old walled city of Dublin. In 1851 the City Administrators took over the building from the Merchants and it houses the Council Chamber for the City Council. In the Members Room, adjoining the Chamber where the City Council meets in committee, three fine Waterford Glass chandeliers were installed some 20 years ago. City Hall can be visited by the public.

Above: Showroom, Waterford Glass head office—Kilbarry, Waterford.

Left: Old Waterford chandelier in Council Chamber, City Hall, Waterford.

The Trophy Gallery

Trophies

Like the sword of Excalibur which granted the grace of knighthood by the tap of its blade, similarly does a Waterford trophy transfer its mystique to the recipient.

In the same sense, the great event or deed which inspires the award transfers its awe to the trophy itself, layering it with a continuing mythology.

In contemporary times, the span of human affairs touched by Waterford trophies is virtually as multi-faceted as the crystal itself. It ranges across the arts, matters of state, sports, industry, the sciences.

Six American presidents—Dwight Eisenhower, John F. Kennedy, Lyndon B. Johnson, Richard M. Nixon, Jimmy Carter, and Ronald Reagan—celebrated their ascendancy by accepting Waterford trophies.

When Dr. Maclyn McCarty won the first Waterford Bio-Medical Science Award in 1977, his audience included Dr. James Watson and Sir Francis Crick, hailed as two of the greatest biologists of the 20th century for their discovery of the DNA structure.

Whether it is England's Queen Mother presenting the Waterford trophy to jockey Willie Carson at Ascot, or Nobel Laureate Baruj Banacerraf accepting the Waterford Award before an audience of his peers, the event is marked by a reciprocal transference of mystique from trophy to man and back again.

Left: Actress Kim Novak, seen here on the set of 'Of Human Bondage' at Ardmore Studios near Dublin, is surrounded by a table setting of Waterford crystal. Above: Dublin's Lord Mayor Ben Briscoe presents President Dwight D. Eisenhower with a Waterford decanter and vase. The photo was taken in the late 1950's.

Left: Irish Ambassador William P. Fay presenting a Waterford Crystal bowl to President Lyndon B. Johnson. Below: Queen Magrethe II of Denmark on a tour of the Waterford factory during a 1978 state visit to Ireland. On her right is Patrick McGrath, Sr.

Left: Bing Crosby and Mrs. Crosby admire the Crosby Tournament trophy.

Left: Queen Elizabeth II of England, in a photograph taken some years ago, is seen with part of the Waterford crystal given her by the Government of Canada.

Above: In 1961, Dublin Lord Mayor Ben Briscoe presented President John F. Kennedy with a Waterford Crystal bowl. Right: President Carter with Dr. Garrett FitzGerald, former Irish Ambassador to the United States who was elected Prime Minister in July, 1981. Below: First Lady Patricia Nixon holding the Waterford vase presented to her and President Nixon by Irish Ambassador William P. Fay.

Top: In the oval office of the White House, sitting in his famous rocking chair and with a Waterford bowl on his table, President Kennedy confers with Secretary of State Dean Rusk, Vice-President Lyndon B. Johnson, and two visiting diplomats. Above: President Ronald Reagan leads a 1981 cabinet meeting with his ever-present vase of jelly beans sitting on the conference table. Left: In a picture taken during the mid 1970's Waterford Crystal's Chairman Patrick W. McGrath (left) and Managing Director Noel Griffin present Prime Minister Jack Lynch with a set of Waterford crystal given to the Irish Government.

Martina Navratilova and Billie Jean King

Chris Evert Lloyd

Tennis tournaments throughout the world
give trophies of engraved Waterford Crystal.
Here are a few of the winners.

Jimmy Connors

Martina Navratilova

John McEnroe

Right: Professional golfer Isao Aoki accepting the trophy for 1978 World Match Play tournament held in Britain. Below: Mr. and Mrs. Andy Bean with the Kemper Open golf tournament trophy and suite of Waterford crystal. Bottom left: Two of the Crosby boys on hand at the family-sponsored tournament. Bottom center: Pat Boone, frequent participant in the Pro-Am division of the Crosby. Bottom right: The beautiful Kemper Open trophy up close.

Top: Actor Rod Taylor wields a huge piece of crystal, hot from re-heating in the furnace, during a factory tour at Waterford. Above: Spanish golfer Severiano Ballesteros, winner of the 1976 Laurent Perrier trophy. Above left: Tom Watson at Pebble Beach. Left: Another beautiful trophy, with the unmistakable Waterford Crystal cutting.

Left: Mrs. Josephine Bothway receives the Waterford Jockeys' Jumping Championship award from the late John Wuidart, then Chairman of Waterford Crystal's U.K. distributors, J. Wuidart & Co. Ltd. Below left: Mrs. Michael Gillow, wife of the Chairman and Managing Director of Aynsley China (who is also a Director of Waterford Crystal), presents a trophy to Mr. L.S. Ivens for Waterford Show Hunter of the Year. Below: The Queen Mother of England presents jockey Willie Carson with the Ritz Trophy during a racing meet at Ascot.

Top: Naomi James, famous for her sailing voyage around the world, traces her journey on a Waterford Crystal globe during a visit to company headquarters in Ireland. Above: Mr. and Mrs. Lamar Hunt with the NFL Hall of Fame trophy. In the center is John Hughes, sports consultant for Waterford. Left: Waterford's Tommy Wall shows former heavyweight boxing champion Floyd Patterson one of the company's engraved trophies.

Dr. Henry G. Kunkel (left) and Dr. Baruj Benacerraf, recipients of the 1980 Waterford Bio-Medical Science Award, inspect their trophies. Both men are immunologists. Dr. Benacerraf was also the 1980 winner of the Nobel Prize for Medicine and Physiology.

Top: The 1978 winner of the Waterford Bio-Medical Science Award, Dr. Neils Jerne, shows off his trophy to students in his Swiss classroom. Right: Dr. Maclyn McCarty greets Nobel laureates Sir Francis Crick (right) and Dr. James Watson.

Top: Dr. Keith R. Porter receives the 1979 award from Waterford's U.S. President, John Miller, as Dr. Frank J. Dixon, Director of Scripps Clinic & Research Foundation, looks on. Left: The Waterford Bio-Medical Science Award was established in 1977 and is given annually in recognition of outstanding achievement in the fields of science and medicine. It is administered by the Scripps Clinic and Research Foundation in La Jolla, California, and includes a $10,000 cash prize in addition to the Waterford Crystal trophy. Above: Dr. Maclyn McCarty accepts the first annual Waterford Bio-Medical Science Award from Harry Pesin at a 1977 banquet in San Diego, California. Left: The Waterford Bio-Medical Science Award trophy up close.

Index

Italicized numbers refer to illustrations and photographs.

Photo credits: Pages 8-57—National Museum of Ireland, Ulster Museum, Trustees of Trinity College, Sotheby's (Ireland), Walter Pfeiffer.

Pages 58-81—Walter Pfeiffer.

Pages 82-167—Terry Murphy, David Howe, Sam Varnedoe.

Pages 168-187—Walter Pfeiffer.

Pages 188-207—Terry Murphy, David Howe.

Pages 208-223—Ira Mandelbaum.

Pages 224-239—Louis Peterse, Jack Buxbaum, Sam Varnedoe.

Pages 240-253—Terry Murphy, Russ Adams, Adler & Associates, Carol L. Newsom, Steve Powell, Frank Johnston/ The Washington Post, Gerry M. Sandford.

Special Notice To Readers

We deeply regret to announce that, as this book went to press, Mr. Noel Griffin drowned while swimming near Dunmore East, Co. Waterford. At the time of his death, Mr. Griffin was Managing Director of Waterford Crystal, Ltd.